Kids in Cults: Why They Join,
Why They Stay, Why They Leave

by
Jack Nusan Porter, Ph.D.,
& Irvin Doress, Ed.D.

Also included are:

Jews & the Cults

Compiled & Annotated by
Jack Nusan Porter, Ph.D.

&

Handbook of Cults, Sects,
& Self-Realization Groups

Compiled by
Jack Nusan Porter, Ph.D.

The Spencer Press
Newton, Mass.

New combined edition © 2014
by The Spencer Press and Jack Nusan Porter
ISBN: 978-0-932270-02-3

The Spencer Press
79 Walnut Street, Unit 4
Newton, MA 02460-1331
(617) 965-8388
jack.porter1@verizon.net

CONTENTS

Introduction to the New Edition

The idea for this combined edition came to me due to a student of mine. He was from Korea but was not Korean, but an American and a "Moonie," a member of the Unification Church founded by Rev. Sun Myung Moon (1920-2012). His name was Gunnard Johnston, a tall Swede around 65 years old. He was an unconventional fellow, but there was something "mystical" about him. I had never spoken to a "Moonie" so candidly before. He intrigued me to come out with a new edition of my three most important works on cults.

Cults in general go through stages: they become what the great German sociologist Max Weber called the "routinization of charisma," that is, they go through stages of conformity from cult to sect to mainstream religion, perhaps retaining some elements of the cult but eventually becoming acceptable to society. The Mormons and Seventh-Day Adventists are good examples. Still, there are lingering doubts and fears about these transformational movements, as there were with the Mormons, especially when Mitt Romney ran for president in 2012.

The same is true for the Unification Church and other cults that have become sects. Some conform better than others. Groups like Scientology still retain fear and loathing; others, like certain meditational Indian cults, have become almost mainstream and non-threatening. I would put the Unification Church somewhere in the middle.

A second influence is that religious groups in general have become very important in our dangerous and chaotic world and still attract, for good or ill, many adherents. I am speaking here of Muslim terrorist groups, but others, less dangerous, are also threatening in one way or another. I speak here, for example, of fundamentalist Hasidic groups or some Christian sects.

A third, less crucial factor may have been my trip to Korea in 2008 and to the Middle East over the past four years — to Egypt, Northern Iraq, Turkey, Israel, Cyprus, and the West Bank/Palestine. I have seen with my own eyes the scourge of genocide and the fear, as well as the defiance, in the eyes of threatened minorities such as Palestinian Christians, Iraqi Kurds, Egyptian Copts, and Lebanese Armenians. Soon the Middle East may be empty of Christians in general. So, religions, for good or evil, are always with us and are always fascinating to study sociologically.

Kids in Cults went through many printings, and was especially popular after Rev. Jim Jones and the People's Temple suicides in the late 1970s. Irv and I were invited everywhere for interviews on TV and in national journals. It was the heyday of cult interest.

I thank Irv Doress, Doris Gold, Meir Rosenberg, and all of those anonymous cult members who talked to us. I must also say that some of these addresses are dated and some may not exist. This is a snapshot of a time in history, and, while most of these cults are still around, their emphasis and location may have changed.

I welcome your comments.

Prof. Jack Nusan Porter

Harvard University - (617) 965-8388

April 1, 2014

Kids in Cults:
Why They Join,
Why They Stay, Why They Leave

By
**Jack Nusan Porter, Ph.D.,
& Irvin Doress, Ed.D.**

Kids in Cults: Why They Join, Why They Stay, Why They Leave

I. Introduction

America has always been a country that has attracted and nurtured religious independence. In many ways we are a very religious nation, but we have a history of both tolerance and bias toward new religions. Founded as a haven from religious persecution, America has also had a history of tolerance: the persecution of the Mormons and Seventh-Day Adventists, attacks against Christian Scientists and Jehovah's Witnesses, and discrimination against Irish Catholics, Pennsylvania Amish and Russian Jews. Some, like the Mormons and the Christian Scientists, started out as sects or "cults" but later became respected and respectable religions in America.

From the early Christians on, there are numerous examples of persecuted sects that later emerged as established churches. We raise this point in order to place some perspective on the current issue. Certain cults and sects have recently come under attack in both the press and the courtroom. Parents and educators have charged cults with everything from brainwashing to sexual orgies, from world domination to satanic violence. There are many myths and half-truths about contemporary sects and cults and, too often, generalizations are made about all cults that should apply only to some. This report, based on interviews with cult participants and participant observation of their places of worship and study, will hopefully shed some light on this fascinating but controversial subject. We are dealing with a large number of highly complex religious phenomena, and must guard against emotional pre-judgment and over-generalization.

It is estimated that in the United States today there are approximately one million people, most of them between eighteen and twenty-five, who have abandoned their traditional American lifestyles in order to become members of one of the approximately 5,000 religious sects and cults in America.[1] These so-called "kids" (most cult followers, while young, are legally adults) can be found in groups ranging from Krishna Consciousness (Hare Krishna) to Jesus People ("Jesus Freaks"); from the Unification Church ("Moonies") to the "Divine Wisdom" of Mahari-ji; from the Children of God to "The Way." Some are unified, highly controlled, centralized, and international in scope, such as the Unification Church of Reverend Sun Myung Moon. Some are decentralized and amorphous, such as the "Jesus Freaks." Cults and sects can be found in every state of the union and in every city, from small towns to large urban centers. Some grow in size (like the "Moonies") and some wane (like the Mahari-ji's group). Some are concentrated in the urban centers of Boston, New York, and San Francisco (like the Hare Krishna); others are more likely to be found in the smaller cities of the Midwest and the South (such as "The Way"). It is a national phenomenon: young people are seeking spiritual renewal in these religious groups. The reasons why may be quite important to this country.

II   *The Characteristics of a Cult*

There are several characteristics that nearly all of the cults we studied share in common:

   a.) An expressive form of worship. These cults are, to use the term from sociology and collective behavior, *expressive movements.* Whereas in most churches strict limits are set on individual expressiveness, in many sects/cults there is an emphasis on exuberance, noise, freedom of movement, and interaction among worshippers. In the established churches' decorum, solemnity, reverence, and humility are emphasized. The distinctive expressiveness of the cults/sects is most attractive to young people. (See Pope, 1942; Broom and Selznick, 1973, 410-420)

   b.) A millennial vision. Most of these groups have some divinely inspired plan for the coming of the Messiah or the "Golden Age," either here on earth or after death. To bring this about, these new "churches" call for the "saving of the world." The Rev. Moon of the Unification Church sums it up best:

> My new revelation has made the will of
> God crystal clear. And what is that will?
> It is to save the world. So the Unification
> Church is not another denomination — it's
> a movement to save the world and through
> the teaching of the word of God, each indi-
> vidual in our movement becomes absolutely
> clear about the concept of the God-cen-
> tered individual, God-centered family, the
> God-centered world. (Quoted in Chesnoff
> and Nagorski, 1976)

   c.) A charismatic leader. Most of these cults/sects have one powerful leader, either a world leader or a local guru. At times these leaders come very close to proclaiming themselves as prophet, or messiah, or even God. Again quoting from the Rev. Moon, who, when asked whether he was a new Messiah, replied:

> We are in a new Messianic age. But 2000 years ago Jesus Christ never spoke of himself as a Messiah, knowing that would not serve his purpose. I am not saying, "I am the Messiah." I am faithfully fulfilling God's instructions. (Chesnoff and Nagorski, 1976)

Rev. Moon may actually be coy. His own followers describe him as a combination of the prophet Elijah and John the Baptist, but if "crucified" and martyred, he could be proclaimed as a new Messiah by his followers. Similar to Mao Tse-Tung, Rev. Moon's followers carry his books with them and study everything he says or does. Many of them believe that he is in fact a "Messiah" already.[2]

d.) *A proselytizing spirit.* Rather than sit home and quietly meditate, most cult/sect members go into the community and, while selling candles, flowers, incense, or booklets, try to reach as many converts as possible by inviting them to have a meal, attend a weekend, study for a week, etc., with the cult.

Unlike Orthodox Hasidic Jews who reach out only to fellow Jews (never Christians), these cults/sects transcend religious differences by going out to Jews, Christians, and atheists alike.

These four basis characteristics emerge from the major American cults we studied. All have an expressive and deeply emotional form of worship, a charismatic leader (The Rev. Sun Myung Moon of the Unification Church, A.C.D. Bhaktivedanta Swami Prabhupada of the Hare Krishna Movement-ISKON-International Society for

Krishna Consciousness, Moses David of the Children of God, the Mahari-ji of the Divine Light Mission, Hannah Lowe of the New Testament Missionary Fellowship, etc.), a millennial vision, and a missionary spirit.

III   Cults, Sects, and Churches

What is the difference between a cult, a sect, and a church? Our limited discussion will touch only the surface of a complex and, at times, fine-lined distinction. An established church or denomination is defined as a formal religious organization with an explicit set of beliefs, system of authority, set of rights and obligations, and a position in society that is by and large accepted and respected by that society. A church is essentially "conservative," in the sense that it stays with what is familiar and shuns sudden and fundamental change and innovation. Of course, churches do change; they are often forced to change by the emergence and breaking away of sects within the church, but they are usually quite deliberate and careful about such change.

A sect, on the other hand, is a religious group that has formed in protest against another group, usually the "mother" church. It represents a set of beliefs and practices that are seen as a return to an earlier and purer form of worship. Sects are usually innovative agencies of change (see Talmon, 1962) both within the church and in society as a whole. Many sects emerge as radical departures, and then become established and respected churches themselves, e.g., the early Christian sects. In America, the early Quakers, Methodists, Adventists, Pentecostals, and Christian Scientists are examples of sects that have become churches. Today, we would suggest, the Hare Krishna, Unification Church, and Jesus People are actually sects, not cults, even though they have certain cultic traits and are sometimes referred to as cults in this report and in other sociological literature.

A cult is a structured and generally small, secretive and esoteric religious group, usually with a charismatic leader, a mystical nature, and a strong sense of isolation and alienation from the general society. It is also the most ephemeral of religious groups. Cults vary a great deal. Some are mild and intellectual, like Theosophy; some have strange and erotic rituals, like the Church of Satan; a very tiny number are violent and, usually, short-lived, such as the Charles Manson cult in California in the early seventies.

Some groups are called cults because they are seen as "weird" or practicing "strange" rituals, with undertones of sexuality and/or violence. The word "cult," being pejorative, is used as a way of negating and diminishing the influence of a religious group, but many so-called cults are really sects or denominational offshoots of established religions. What makes them seem "cultic" is that they have charismatic leaders, emanate from foreign lands (Korea, Japan, China, India, etc.), and have customs that are little known to Westerners. The Hare Krishna, for example, are an offshoot of Hinduism, a legitimate Hindu denomination; the Black Muslims and the Hanafi Moslems are offshoots of Islam (though some might quarrel with this); the various "yogis" and "swamis" are representative of either Indian or Japanese Buddhism; the "Moonies" are really offshoots of the Christian Church in Korea and Japan.

Parents and educators, abetted by misinformed intellectuals and writers, often label some groups as sects or cults when in fact they are not, though they may share such similarities as a charismatic leader and an esoteric set of techniques. They are not cults because (1) they publicly admit that they are not a religion, (2) they accept people of all religions and do not ask them to convert, and (3) they do not pray to a deity and do not ask their followers to pray to any particular god. These groups are usually psychological or meditative societies, not cults. Psycho-synthesis, Rolfing, EST (Erhard Seminars Training), acupuncture, Esalen, Fischer-Hoffman psychic therapy, etc., are not cults. Transcendental meditation and various yogas (e.g., the Integral Yoga Institute) are relaxation techniques, and not cults, even though these techniques can be used in a religious setting. (See the attached list of cults, sects, and self-improvement techniques.)

IV   Why Do They Join?

Why do young people join cults? Our research indicates that it is mainly young adults of post-high school age who are attracted, and not older, established families with children and careers. This fact alone tells us a great deal about their reasons for joining.

a) *To find a family.* The Unification Church constantly emphasizes the breakdown of the American family, corruption and immorality in American life (divorce, pornography, suicide, drugs, and scandal), and, by contrast, the work of the church toward the "perfect family" in a "perfect world. The stress on the family is so pervasive that one cult calls itself "The Love Family," while others call themselves "The Family" or "Love Israel."

Family life in America is beset by conflicts and problems. A great many families espouse a set of workably good values, but they live their lives by a contradictory value set. When the progeny of such families see such contradictions, they begin to search out and seek answers from their parents. If the "answers" are not forthcoming, or are of a poor quality, the children may start looking elsewhere. They may look to "surrogate" families to meet their needs. Recent research has shown that American parents do a great deal of psychological and physical violence to their children.[3] Many youths may be improving themselves by joining cults/sects and moving from a negative, hurting environment to one characterized by ego-support, non-belligerence, and persuasion rather than force.

b) *The search for answers, a spiritual search.* Children reared in mature, established religions are used to *not* getting answers to their questions. This can lead to a sense of incompleteness and dissatisfaction. When a cult comes along and offers definitive and complete answers, it is very tempting for the youngsters to be caught up in the lifestyles of the answer-givers. Early phases of religions tend to be fanatical and full of "perfect" answers.

Often the religion of the parents is nonexistent, or so part-time that it is totally ineffectual. The children see through this meaninglessness, and therefore seek a religion that offers meaning, structure, and full-time commitment. They desire religion as *a way of life*, not as a sometime thing.

c) *Security.* Though we need more research to bear this out, a significant percentage of families in our society seem to be afflicted by marital discord, marital breakdown, intergenerational strife, gross immaturities, and child/adolescent abuse, all of which can lead to a sense of insecurity. What does one do when one is insecure? A variety of things, one of which is to look for a replacement family. Cults/sects often act as such secure "homes," even more secure than the political and cultural groupings of the 1960s.

d) *Differentiation.* According to Gail Sheehy's seminal and original treatise *Passages* (1976), young people crave differentiation from their parents. If this is so, then the form that such adolescent rebellion can take is association with cults. In our interviews with cult "devotees," we found that they tried to rebel in various ways (drugs, promiscuity, running away, etc.) before turning to the cults. Examples of differentiation offered by the cults include:

- a religion that is totally different

- communal living vs. nuclear family

- spirituality vs. materialism

- austerity vs. extravagant spending

- a different culture and subculture

- a different set of customs and traditions

- a different set of attitudes

- a different set of clothing, hairstyles, etc.

All of these differences constitute what one may call the process of differentiation that marks the period of growing up. It is a way to detach oneself from parental values and develop a new and vastly different value set.

e) *Adolescent rebellion.* Closely aligned with differentiation, adolescent rebellion is a concomitant of advanced Western industrial society. It takes many forms: panty raids, rushing into the Marines at fifteen, smoking marijuana, alcoholic binges, riding the rails, living like a hobo, wrecking the family car, taking off, and, finally, joining a cult. Being in a successful cult can be a great opportunity to look out of the corner of the eye and say about one's parents: "Look at what they are doing, and look at what I'm into. I'm so mad at them and their foul-ups. While they are about to go over Niagara Falls in a barrel, I'm approaching my zenith."

Although permissiveness is not the major culprit leading to rebellion that certain political and religious groups rail about, we would speculate that some young people rebel against structure-lessness or over-permissiveness, or what sociologists call alienation or anomie. They find it anxiety provoking and therefore go off to find such structure in a cult. The cult will represent a rebellion against all they knew before. It will provide the structure and content they seek. Often, there is a complete turnabout, for example, from promiscuity to celibacy or from lack of self-control to tight control.

f) *Adventure.* Ever since Huckleberry Finn and Tom Sawyer, boys and girls have longed for adventure. Whether it is going to the candy store or the movies without Mommy's approval or running away from home at age fourteen, there is something exciting about the risk. Adventure contains elements of both rebellion and differentiation. In addition, it may represent an escape from boredom, strict parents, or onerous duties at home. Also, a person who seems relatively unsuccessful at trying to emulate a father who is a factory worker in Lowell, Massachusetts, or Milwaukee, Wisconsin, could "take off" and join a cult. In a few years that youngster could enter the leadership ranks of the cult. In this sense, cults may even be a form of upward mobility in an economically stagnant society.

g) *Attention.* One of the basic needs promulgated by sociologist W.I. Thomas is recognition. When we speak of attention or the desire for attention, we are speaking at least partly of recognition. The cults seem to be a shortcut method of achieving instant attention and recognition. In the Unification Church devotees are even taught how to smile at people. All guests are warmly welcomed. In a harsh urban landscape, this can prove almost irresistible to newcomers. Furthermore, as a devotee, one is visible and differentiated. The response from the general public may be negative, but at least it is a response of some kind; such individuality is very satisfying to youth in cults seeking attention, recognition, and even notoriety. The saffron robes of the Hare Krishna and the rough cloth robes of the Children of God are attention-getting. It is a way of saying: "Here I am, whether you like it or not. I exist. And you'd better listen, or the world will come to an end!"

h) Idealism. In one case we know the daughter attempted to replicate in a generic way her father's idealism. He was quite active in civil rights and peace movements. For this she admired him, but she had to do things in her own way. Ultimately she joined the Hare Krishna group because one of the major goals of the Krishnas (and many other cults/sects) is to bring about world peace. Of course, the cult's approach to peace is to convert everyone to its way of thinking. This is similar to the *Pax Americana*, which the late President Kennedy warned against, by which everything in the world is relentlessly converted to America, Americanism, and American culture. In any event, many people join cults for such idealistic reasons.

i) Under-employment and dead-end jobs. There are probably few things as depressing or frightening as losing one's job and entering the ranks of the unemployed. Panic may set in, and an individual may take precipitous steps. Some go into serious depression. At any rate, an unemployed young man or woman may opt to join a cult. At least, such people have a roof over their heads and free meals in return for begging in the streets 12-14 hours a day. At best, they could move up the hierarchy of the cult into a position of responsibility and status.

V   Why Do They Stay?

Once they have joined the cult, why do young people stay in?

a) *Needs being met.* Whatever needs brought them
   in (security, rebellion, recognition, idealism) will
   also make them stay. For example, if they go in to
   obtain security and find it, why should they leave?
   They may not leave, and it will take a very per-
   suasive argument to convince them to do so. And
   whether we abhor cults or not, a number of them
   do in fact meet the needs of many of their followers.

b) *Good, loving interpersonal relations.* Whether people
   are in the Navy, at home with parents, or in a cult,
   good loving relationships will tend to sustain them
   and make them want to remain in the institution —
   and not "jump ship." This is one of the reasons that
   cults are difficult to fight — they are hard to replace in this crucial area of loving care. People will
   not leave unless the cult changes or they begin to
   see the true nature of it, i.e., that it is *not* so loving
   and caring after all.

c) *A finer, purer physical and moral environment.* In the
   face of the moral decay of a society characterized by
   alcoholism, drug abuse, promiscuity, and violence,
   the cults are in a position to offer an environment
   that is alcohol-free, drug-free, violence-free, and
   virtually sex-free. Although a small number of cults
   have been accused of using drugs as well as practicing promiscuity and sexual orgies (in America this
   has historically been a popular — and sometimes
   truthful — denunciation), we have found that the
   major cults (Moonies, Krishnas, Scientology, The
   Way) tend to be quite puritanical regarding affairs
   of the flesh. Sex is forbidden unless one is married,
   and then only for procreation. Drugs and alcohol
   are also strictly forbidden as harmful to the body.
   Furthermore, the physical environment of the
   church and *ashram* is closely guarded. The Krishna
   ashram is cleaned every day and is spotless. Many

15

cults have moved or hope to move to the country in order to find a purer environment. Many already have country retreats, but stay in the city because potential converts are there in great numbers. Most cults seek an environment that is clean internally (mind, soul, and body) and externally (home, air, water, food).

d) *Spiritual hunger.* The thing that brings hundreds of American youth into the cults in the first place also tends to keep them involved. Once the spiritual need is filled, it becomes habit-forming. Spiritual "trips" are more addictive and more "powerful" than most drugs. There is a great deal of pleasure derived from chanting, dancing, and speaking in tongues. We also suggest that to a certain extent it is sexual sublimation.

e) *Fear of leaving.* Cult leaders claim that their followers are free to leave at any time. This is both true and false. While not forcibly restrained, it has been our observation that many devotees are told that if they leave or deviate from the "party line" God will punish them or their parents, or they will be crippled for life, afflicted by a dread disease, cursed, or even die. They are sometimes told that their parents and friends are "devils" and that their only true salvation is to stay in the cult. Thus physical restraint is unnecessary. "Spiritual" persuasion is a way of keeping subjects in the cult, and it is quite effective.

The security and ego-support offered by the cult is hard to find on the outside. Therefore, devotees are often afraid to leave because they fear lack of these qualities in the outside world. They fear making a total readjustment to the world. We have found that a small but constant number of devotees have some form of mental illness. In some cases, the cult acts as a benign and supportive "mental hospital" for these kids, better than many public institutions. The cult allows these young people to act out their psychosis in a spiritual way. This fascinating issue should be studied more. There are, of course, devotees who leave the cult but still believe in many of its teachings. Such believers become householders, living in an apartment nearby and attending functions at the cult center. This appears to be a compromise with the full-time demands of the cult.

VI Why Do They Leave?

Many of the parents with whom we have talked have given up hope that their children will ever leave the cult. There are ways, whether by choice or by force, by which young people leave.

a) *Disillusionment.* We do not know the attrition rate from cults (it undoubtedly varies), but inevitably some devotees become disillusioned by the gap between promise and reality within the cult. They feel that they will never achieve their goal of "saving the world." Some give up hope; others lose patience; still others find life in the cult too difficult to maintain. Also, youngsters may have a genuine change of heart and leave. There have been a few cases of poor nutrition, inadequate health precautions, and similar factors that have induced some to leave.

b) *Completion of stage of development.* Some young people go into cults, like into the army, to fulfill certain developmental tasks. When these are accomplished, and the child recognizes it, he or she may decide to leave. If there is no undue fear of leaving the cult, they will, in fact, leave on their own. It is a fact that most cult followers are young people. As they grow older they may find the cult/

sect useful in their lives and remain, or they may learn from it and leave when they have completed this stage of development, taking with them some interesting experiences and valuable lessons.

c) *Kidnap-rescue.* This seems to us the most unnatural and most dangerous way of leaving, but in a few cases it may be the only way for parents to regain their children. Some devotees "ask" their parents to remove them forcibly by various cues, doubletalk, or non-verbal expression. Subjects who have been taken out this way often go later to therapists for help. It is impossible to state whether they went to a psychologist or a psychiatrist because of the nature of the release from the cult or due to earlier problems. It is more likely that being in a cult for any amount of time has its traumatic effects and, then again, the readjustment period to the "straight" world is also a factor. The kidnapping methods of Ted Patrick and others can be expensive, illegal, and not always effective, despite their claims.

It must be pointed out that some young people do not want to return or cannot return home. They may even be homeless, "orphans" in a sense. The cult may then become their family and, if it falls apart, they may seek other cults. We could call these people "cult addicts," serving a protean function of experimentation and existential trial and error.

VII *What Can Parents and Educators Do?*

There are several things that parents and educators can do in response to either the general phenomenon of young people in cults or the particular dilemma of having one's child in a cult. It is important to know as much as possible about the cult or sect, to meet with devotees, to visit their meeting place, and to understand their philosophy and teachings. Each cult, each situation, must be treated individually. Counselors, teachers, and social workers must know first-hand the nature of the cult and its relationship to the child before any steps are taken. Here are some possible approaches that concerned individuals should consider:

a) *Kidnap-rescue.* This action, as indicated above, is most controversial, and contains within it an entangled series of ethical, legal, psychological and physical aspects. To kidnap one's own child, despite the conditions within a cult, is an application of force. A basic law of physics states that the child may trigger a violent counter-response, such as armed or unarmed resistance, counter-kidnapping, etc. Despite all claims to the contrary, kidnapping is dangerous and risky. The response of the child or adult to the kidnapping will vary — perhaps positive, perhaps negative, depending on the success of the subsequent deprogramming and rehabilitation.

Ted Patrick, once a public relations aide to former Governor Ronald Reagan of California, is the best known and probably the most effective rescuer-deprogrammer. He charges a great deal of money, depending on the amount of assistance, airfare and time needed to deprogram. In the past judges have been lenient on Patrick, but recently a judge in Denver sentenced him to two years for kidnapping. (He has appealed.) Other deprogrammers, such as Joe Alexander of Ohio and Michael Trauscht of Tucson, Arizona, have also entered the field. Patrick claims 95-98% success, but we do not trust his figures. We know of several Boston-area cases that have been "botched up." Parents and educators are well advised to think of this approach as a last resort. It is filled with risk.

The courts may eventually rule that it is uncon-
stitutional to "kidnap" an adult (non-minor) son
or daughter unless the young person is in perilous
danger, and "perilous danger" will be hotly debated by pro- and anti-cult forces.

b) *Conservatorship.* Some parents have been able to
obtain "conservatorship" of their children. Akin to
guardianship, this allows the parents to obtain legal
right to keep the child (adult) under their control.
In a closed court hearing parents, lawyers, and doc-
tors argue that the cult follower is a "helpless victim of mind control." If the judge agrees, a pickup
can be made with the help of law-enforcement
agents. Consistent with their view of kidnapping,
civil libertarians and like-minded people seriously
question the constitutionality of such procedures.

c) *Seeking counseling from specialists.* Around the country there are a number of organizations created
by parents, social workers, and concerned citizens
which offer counseling, workshops, advice, and the
like. They have such names as Return to Personal
Choice, Committee Engaged in Freeing Minds,
Citizens Engaged in Reuniting Families, and similar titles. The helpers in their organizations are fre-
quently parents of cult/sect members or ex-cultists
themselves. Some of these groups, however, will
not allow psychologists or social workers to counsel
parents and children if they have a son or daughter
in a cult. They feel that this affects the "objectivity"
of the counselor. There are also individual psychia-
trists, psychologists, social workers, and counselors
who have developed a specialty in this area.

Some of these helpers and organizations look
favorably upon rescue-deprogramming; others are
neutral or discourage its use. Individuals who have

had some experience with cults are often more effective than trained professionals who often know little of this specialized area. It is a new subject in the mental health field, and many professionals, despite their experience, know very little about cults. Counselors, therefore, must be chosen with care. Furthermore, we have found that it is the parents who may be in need of counseling or therapy as much as the child.

d) *Live and let live.* Not all parents are against cults. Quite a number accept the differences between their own beliefs and those of their children. These parents are likely to be open and tolerant in their thinking. They are parents who believe in cultural relativism, that there is some good in all beliefs. They are parents who are not only not religious themselves but who may even be atheists.

If, for a moment, one were to examine cults objectively, one might see that there are many things worse than joining a cult. Most of the cults we have studied are strongly against drugs, alcohol, smoking, gambling, promiscuity, and dishonesty in any form. They preach love and respect for each other and for their country and community. There are groups, however, that utilize "heavenly deception" on others, and who think that non-believers are lost and ignorant at best and the "devil incarnate" at worst. But despite this, there is *some good* in *some* cults. There is also some evidence that where there is parental acceptance of the cult, a fair amount of social interaction between parent and child may occur. Although parents may become bored with cult-dominated or cult-obsessed conversations, there is at least a modicum of communication with the child.

e) *Fighting religion with religion.* It stands to reason that if most cult members leave home to become more spiritual, then infusing more religion into the home might conceivably impress the young people and bring them back.

A friendly, even spirited, discussion of religion can take place in the context of a warm visit between the child and parents in the cult's church or *ashram*, at the parent's home, or in a neutral setting. If tempers remain calm, if the parental case is convincing, and if the devotee's case is weak, the child could be won back if the time spent in the cult hasn't been too long. On the other hand, if the devotee's case is stronger, an impasse may occur, or the parents will display a more accepting attitude toward the cult, or become "converted" themselves to the cult. When such a religious "debate" takes place, anything can happen.

Charismatic, evangelistic, highly emotional, involving, and family-centered religions are, in our judgment, very effective in bringing young people back from the cults, but any *bona fide* religion can be effective. When you remove someone from a cult, you must have a replacement. If no other religion is found, then the child may nosedive back into the cult.

The replacement could be Hasidism for Jews, evangelical Baptist or Campus Crusade for Christ for Protestants, or a more involved form of Catholicism for Catholics. Hasidism and its moral equivalents in Christianity make excellent halfway houses or even permanent homes for cult refugees. Such religions are usually "full-time." While they may not involve the person for twenty-four hours a day, they are more than just one-day-a-week religions. They offer greater spiritual involvement, which is what many young people are seeking. If they do not find it in their home, church, or synagogue, they may go after it in the cults.

f) Wait for the effects of time. If parents reject the suggestions offered above, there may be little they can do except to visit, communicate, and keep the door open. Children *do* leave cults on their own. There is little data on exactly how many leave, but some undoubtedly do — for the reasons noted above. In 1972, a Boston student we know wanted to leave a cult called "The Family." She was advised by cult members that they would break her leg "for her own good" if she tried. She got some "tough guys" from her hometown to help her move, and no legs were broken. She has never gone back.

We recommend an open attitude. Becoming infuriated and acting hysterically, a common reaction among the parents, will not bring the child back any sooner. In fact, just the opposite may occur. Our advice to parents is to attempt some deep introspection into the motives of their child and to try to find out why their child decided to join a cult. They may learn some valuable things about themselves as well. One should also learn as much as possible about the cult/sect by reading the literature, visiting the church or *ashram*, and keeping open the lines of communication. The counseling involved is quite sensitive and complex.

VIII Conclusion

In this paper we have described in brief the characteristics which distinguish a cult, a sect, and a church. We have shown how cults may be a vehicle for radical social change of an internal or spiritual nature, as opposed to radical political movements which attempt change of an external nature.[4] Some cults attempt to achieve both. We have also suggested why young people join cults, why they stay, and why they leave. We have concluded with some ideas about what parents and educators can do.

Every age in history has had religious movements that are born, mature, and pass. Our age is no exception. Cults are not new. They will persist. What can be done about them? What can we learn from them? Some experts suggest that a child must be removed from the cult as quickly as possible and as forcibly as necessary. Educating people about the nature of cults is very important. Education, some feel, may be the most effective method in combating cults. Others insist that we must offer young children "dramatic" and appealing alternatives. Parents and educators must come together in order to choose the techniques and alternatives listed above that best fit the situation of their child, school, or community.

Notes

[1] These data are derived both from the cults themselves, which exaggerate their numbers, and anti-cult experts such as Patrick and Dulack (1976), who also exaggerate. All figures are approximate. No one has exact data because membership fluctuates, and most cults are so small and secretive (less than 25 people) that even the researchers are not aware of them. We are constantly discovering new cults in various parts of the country.

[2] This leads to the fascinating question of charisma building and charisma transference. What will happen when Rev. Moon dies? Who will succeed him? This is a common problem and a common fate among most cults. They often falter and diminish because no leader can be found to replace the one with charisma. (See Weber, 1968)

[3] See the writings of Suzanne K. Steinmetz and Murray Straus (1974) on violence in the American family, as well as recent governmental reports.

[4] For an example of the interplay between religion and politics, see Porter and Dreier (1973). Religion often provides the thrust and structure for powerful political change.

<u>REFERENCES</u>

There is a small but important body of literature dealing with the cults and sects. In the general studies of cults
as seen from the perspective of social movements, there
is the collective behavior research of Zaretsky and Leone
(1974), Lanternari (1963), Wallace (1956), Cantril (1941),
Meyer (1965), Hoffer (1951), Toch (1965), Turner and
Killian (1972), and Rudavsky (1972). For more specific
studies of cults there are Griswold (1934), Beynon (1938),
Black (1977), Cox (1977), Eister (1972), Oeschger (1977),
Patrick and Dulack (1976), Orrmont (1961), Robbins and
Dick (1972), and Deutsch (1975). For studies of the Hare
Krishna, see Levine (1974); for the Unification Church
of the Rev. Moon, see Lofland (1966), Lofland and Stark
(1965), Rice (1976), Lynch (1977), Robbins, Dick and
Doucas (1976), and Horowitz (1977).

The booklets, "bibles," holy writing, and magazines of
the cults also contain valuable information, as do the popular media (*Newsweek, Readers Digest, Harpers, Saturday
Evening Post*), the Sunday editions of many newspapers,
and the religious journals (*America, Christianity Today,
Commonweal, Midstream, Jewish Currents*).

Beynon, Erdmann D., "The Voodoo Cult among Negro Migrants in Detroit," *American Journal of Sociology*, Vol. 43 (May 1938), pp. 894-907. Like John Lofland's seminal book on the Unification Church, *Doomsday Cult* (1966), this is one of the first sociological articles on a group that later became known as the Black Muslims.

Black, David, "The Secrets of the Innocents: Why Kids Join Cults," *Woman's Day*, Vol. 40, No. 6, February 1977, pp. 91, 166-175.

Broom, Leonard, and Philip Selznick, *Sociology*, New York: Harper and Row, Fifth Edition, 1973.

Cantril, Hadley, *The Psychology of Social Movements*, New York: John Wiley and Sons, 1973.

Chesnoff, Richard Z., and Andrew Nagorski, "An Interview with Reverend Sun Myung Moon," *Newsweek International*, June 14, 1976.

Cox, Harvey, *Turning East*, New York: Simon & Schuster, 1977.

Deutsch, Alexander, "Observations on a Sidewalk Ashram," *Archives of General Psychiatry*, Vol. 32 (2), Feb. 1975, pp. 166-175.

Eister, Allan W., "An Outline of a Structural Theory of Cults," *Journal for the Scientific Study of Religion*, Vol. 11 (4), Dec. 1972, pp. 319-333.

Fishman, Samuel Z. (ed.), *Jewish Students and the Jesus Movement*, Washington, D.C.: B'nai B'rith Hillel Foundations, 1973.

Griswold, Alfred W., "New Thought: A Cult of Success," *American Journal of Sociology*, Vol. 40 (Nov. 1934), pp. 309-318.

Hoffer, Eric, *The True Believer*, New York: Harper and Row, 1951.

Horowitz, I.L., "Science, Sin, and Sponsorship," *Atlantic Monthly*, Vol. 239, No. 3, March 1977, pp. 98-102.

Lanternari, Vittorio, *The Religions of the Oppressed: A Study of Modern Messianic Cults*, London: MacGibbon and Kee, Ltd., 1963.

Levine, Faye, *The Strange World of the Hare Krishnas*, New York: Fawcett Publications, 1974.

Lofland, John, *Doomsday Cult*, Englewood Cliffs, N.J.: Prentice-Hall, 1966. This is probably the first study of the "Moonies," and a second edition from Irvington Publishers of New York will appear shortly.

Lynch, Frederick R., "Field Research and Future History: Problems Posed for Ethnographic Sociologists by the 'Doomsday Cult' Making Good," *The American Sociologist*, Vol. 12 (2), May 1977, pp. 80-88.

Meyer, Donald, *The Positive Thinkers*, New York: Doubleday, 1965.

Oeschger, Karen, "Cults: Why They Became So Popular in the First Half of the 1970s," unpublished paper, Boston: Simmons College, 1977.

Orrmont, Arthur, *Love Cults and Faith Healers*, New York: Ballantine, 1961.

Patrick, Ted, and Tom Dulack, *Let Our Children Go!*, New York: Dutton, 1976.

Pope, Liston, *Millhands and Preachers*, New Haven, Conn.: Yale University Press, 1942.

Porter, Jack Nusan, and Peter Dreier (eds.), *Jewish Radicalism*, New York: Grove Press, 1973.

Rice, Berkeley, "Messiah from Korea: Honor Thy Father Moon," *Psychology Today*, Vol. 9, Jan. 1976, pp. 36-47.

Robbins, Thomas, and Anthony Dick, "Getting Straight with Meher Baba: A study of mysticism, drug rehabilitation, and post-adolescent role conflict," *Journal for the Scientific Study of Religion*, Vol. II (2), Jan. 1972, pp. 122-140.

Robbins, Thomas, Anthony Dick, and Madeline Doucas, "The Last Civil Religion: Reverend Moon and the Unification Church," *Sociological Analysis*, Vol. 37 (Summer 1976), pp. 111-127.

Rudavsky, David, *Modern Jewish Religious Movements*, New York: Behrman House, 1972.

Sheehy, Gail, *Passages*, New York: E.P. Dutton, 1976.

Spero, Moshe Halevi, "Cults: Some Theoretical and Practical Perspectives," *Journal of Jewish Communal Service*, Vol. 53, No. 4 (Summer 1977), pp. 330-338.

Steinmetz, Suzanne K., and Murray Straus, *Violence in the Family*, New York: Dodd, Mead, and Company, 1974.

Talmon, Yoina, "Pursuit of the Millennium: The Relation Between Religious and Social Change," *Archives Européenes de Sociologie*, (1) 1962, pp. 125-148.

Toch, Hans, *The Social Psychology of Social Movements*, New York: Bobbs-Merrill Company, 1965, especially pp. 56-60.

Turner, Ralph H. and Lewis M. Killian, *Collective Behavior*, Englewood Cliffs, N.J.: Prentice-Hall, 1972, second edition, especially pp. 379-387.

Wallace, Anthony F.C., "Revitalization Movements," *American Anthropologist*, Vol. 58 (April 1956), pp. 268-276.

Weber, Max, *On Charisma and Institution Building*, Chicago: University of Chicago Press, 1968.

Zaretsky, Irving J., and Mark P. Leone, *Religious Movements in Contemporary America*, Princeton, N.J.: Princeton University Press, 1974.

List of Cults, Sects, &
Self-Improvement Techniques

The following list is limited to the major groups and gives only a brief description. Interested readers should pursue books and articles mentioned in the bibliography and write or go directly to the church for more information. Cults and sects are listed first, followed by self-improvement therapies, techniques, and psychologies.

Cults and Sects:

Unification Church — Founded by the Rev. Sun Myung Moon, a Korean missionary, the "Moonies' are an aggressive, Christian, missionizing sect with churches around the world. Its international headquarters are in Barrytown, New York. It also seems to be growing rapidly. Uses a wide variety of "front" organizations.

Krishna Consciousness — Sometimes called the Hare Krishnas after their well-known chant, they are a neo-Hindu sect founded in New York City in 1966, but their leaders come from India. ISKCON, their international society, claims 5,000 members in about 65 locations around the world, with major concentrations in the large

U.S. cities. Krishna is a Hindu deity. Sect members take on Hindu religious names.

Children of God — a "doomsday cult" that preaches the "end of the world" unless people return to Jesus' teaching. Founded in 1968 in the United States under the leadership of Moses David. Cult members take on Biblical names.

The Process — Another "doomsday cult" with overtones of Satanism. Active in the Midwest.

Divine Light Mission — an esoteric cult revolving around a teenaged "perfect master," an Indian by the name of Maharaj-ji. Seems to be losing members.

Jesus People (including *Jews for Jesus, Messianic Jews, B'nai Yeshua*) — evangelical Christian missionaries, active throughout the U.S. The Jews for Jesus, numbering some ten to twenty thousand, are active in major cities from Los Angeles to New York. The majority of their members are probably *not* of Jewish origin.

The Way — a growing, missionizing Christian sect, popular in the South and Midwest.

Theosophy — Mme. Lavatsky, a founder of the Theosophical Society in 1875, defined it as a "wisdom religion or divine wisdom." It differs from Spiritualism in ascribing spirit messages to the activities of "astral shells" or evil spirits. It also teaches a doctrine of compulsory reincarnation and the development of latent psychic powers.

Gurdjieff Method — George I. Gurdjieff (died 1949) was a Greek mystic and writer. He inspired P.D. Ouspensky (born 1878), a Russian student, who in turn developed and spread his message to the West (England and America). The formulated a fourth dimensional philosophy, bringing Western rationalism and Eastern mysticism.

There are many other groups (*Love Israel, The Family, Hannan Lowe's New Testament Missionary Fellowship*, etc.), but these are the major ones.

Self-Improvement Techniques and Therapies:

There are literally hundreds of such techniques, but the following are the ones most people confuse with cults:

EST (Erhard Seminars Training) — Founded by Werner Erhard (*aka* Jack Rosenberg), an American, it is an expensive (over $200), quick (usually four days) method of clearing up such questions as, "Who am I?", "What are my goals?", and other existential questions.

Transcendental Meditation — Encompasses various techniques, but the one developed by the Indian "guru" Maharishi Mahesh Yogi is the most popular. In essence, meditation is a method of sitting, relaxing, and with the help of a mantra (sound), contemplating. It purports to "expand consciousness, increase intelligence, and enable one to use full potential in all fields of thought and action." Also expensive (over $150).

Yoga — Various types of yoga, but all based on an ancient Hindu system of self-discipline and psychic training, using particular breathing and "exercising" methods. The object is to unite "Lower Self" with "Higher Self" and thus attain freedom from an inexorable round of rebirth and Karma (compulsory reincarnation to either higher or lower forms). Yoga is now used as a system of physical culture, but this was not intended.

Scientology — Founded by L. Ron Hubbard, an American, it claims to be a "modern science of mental health." It is also a systematic sociology of knowledge. Through the techniques of "Dianetics," it attempts to uncover memories of previous incarnations. It has close philosophical ties with theosophy. Scientology is quite active in major American cities, and is a psychology that comes close to being a cult, built around the central figure of founder Hubbard.

For help and information, write to:

Reconciliation Associates
Jack Porter
79 Walnut Street, Apt. 4
Newtonville, MA 02460-1331

Citizens Engaged in Reuniting Families
Box 368
Harrison, NY 10528

Committee Engaged in Freeing Minds
Box 5084
Arlington, TX 76011

Citizens' Freedom Foundation
Box 256
Chula Vista, CA 92012

Dr. John Clark
476 Conant Road
Weston, MA 02193
(617) 899-4962

Return to Personal Choice, Inc.
Box 159
Lincoln, MA 01773

THE AUTHORS

Dr. Irvin Doress was an associate professor of educational counseling at Northeastern University in Boston and a psychotherapist. He is the father of a child in the Hare Krishna. He is also a trained psychotherapist and family counselor.

Dr. Jack Nusan Porter is a sociologist and writer, specializing in contemporary religious issues. He has taught Jewish theology at Boston College, Jewish history at Emerson College, general sociology courses at other colleges and universities, and is the author of *Jewish Radicalism* (Grove Press, 1973), *Jews and the Cults* (Biblio Press, 1981), and *Handbook on Cults and Sects* (The Spencer Group, 1984).

The authors can be reached at the following address:
Dr. Jack Nusan Porter
79 Walnut Street, Apt. 4
Newtonville, MA 02460-1331
(617) 965-8388

Special rates for religious schools, community centers, classroom use, etc., in orders of 20 or more.

We welcome your comments and questions.

The authors are also available for speaking engagements on the topic of cults and related issues. Contact The Spencer Group at the above address or call (617) 965-8388 in Newton, Mass.

JEWS & THE CULTS

Compiled & Annotated
by
Jack Nusan Porter, Ph.D.

INTRODUCTION

Jews and Cults (understood essentially as Jews *in* Cults) has recently claimed a greater share of attention from the Jewish community and Jewish families whose members have been attracted to cults. Religious scholars and sociologists have examined cults because, among other effects, cults have become yet another symptom of social change, of disaffection by young people from established religion, and of their preferences for counter-culture behavior.

Particularly since the tragedy of Jonestown in Guyana in November 1978, mountains of material have been written around cult leadership and membership, deprogramming, legal restrictions and brainwashing which are currently still being debated.

This Bibliography and Resource Guide is intended for the reader interested in exploring a limited area of the subject — the recent awareness that Jews, who are only approximately 2.8 percent of the United States population, are also to be found among cult members in these estimated proportions: within the Unification Church (Moonies), 12 percent; Hare Krishna, 20 percent; and the Divine Light Mission, over 25 percent.[1]

There are said to be 1,300 cults (some offer a high of 5,000, depending on definition) in the United States today, claiming a membership of about 1 million, mostly between 18-26 years. The majority are white middle to upper middle class, who come from families with median incomes, many who are educated and suburban. Those from Black or Puerto Rican families living in poverty are in the minority. The cults attract young people and a large number of young women.

Rabbi Maurice Davis,[2] a well-known crusader against cults, explains why: Young people are vulnerable. Their very "goodness" makes them vulnerable. Their search for a better world makes them vulnerable. The typical candidates are college freshmen and women who are naïve, bewildered, lonely or embittered. The cults feed upon these young students and young adults in the population. Older, more mature people, whether married couples or the elderly, have enough ego strength and social supports to ward off the cults. They are less naïve. They have less time and energy to devote to full-time missionary work than a young student or unemployed "drop-out."

One can assume that in most cults or sects, whether Eastern or Western, mystical or pragmatic, quasi-cultic or mainstream, from est to TM, from the most benign to the most "dangerous," one will find some young, searching Jews. Many find it of interest that Jews have always been visible in radical, political, artistic, cultural and religious avant-garde movements since the time they freed themselves from the confining ghettos of Europe and the United States.

Why do they join? This complex question was posed by Rabbi Zalman Schachter, Professor of Jewish Mysticism at Temple University, to a swami. The swami's response was: "You Jews must be a very spiritual people, because SUBUD, Bahai, Vedanta Society, I-AM, Theosophical Society... they're all full of Jews."[3]

It has been noted by some that Jews were among those in Jonestown leadership cliques; that other cults have had Jewish leaders, including the Unification (Moonies) Church. Ironically, there have been relatively fewer Jewish members in cults founded by apostate Jews, such as David Berg's Children of God, the Tony and Susan Alamo Foundation, and The Way International.

It might thus seem that one reason for the cult's appeal to Jews is positive: the search for spiritual values. But the question still remains, why in cults and not in mainstream Judaism? The trend also appears contradictory, because Jews consider themselves in the main to be liberal, progressive, and egalitarian, while most cults are known to be conservative, authoritarian, regimented in group behavior and sexist in their attitudes toward women and children, who are often second-class citizens in cult life. Many cults are apolitical, but others are strongly anti-socialist, anti-abortion, and even anti-sex. To Jewish parents, the attraction of such negative values is deeply puzzling.

Cults are highly demanding of their members, requiring enormous self-sacrifice, which includes the giving of material resources to strangers, the abandonment of careers and friendships. Some are dangerous to one's health because of restricted diets, lack of sleep, "mind-control" and allegiance to one's leader. This total commitment demand is framed in "family feeling," surrogates of "sisters and brothers" — strangers with artificial warmth, who appear to provide a structure for living.

Some Jewish cult youth have said that their former family Judaism was too intellectual, too cerebral — that the rich, emotional forms were missing, as well as the intimate connection between historical events and everyday life. Others want a religion "on the move," a transforming spirit that will change themselves and their world. Some have seen Judaism as restricted to synagogue life and holidays which do not inspire one's being. (Those in search of 24-hour religious observance were obviously unaware of Lubavitch or Satmar Chassidism.) Others have expressed rejection of Judaism and its perceived parochial materialism and concern for status.

Cults are more likely to be understood as the "radical politics" of the 1970s, or the reaction-formation of the drug counterculture of the 1960s. Many have observed that uncompetitive youth drift either into drugs or into esoteric cults — a retreat from political or personal action as a solution. The Marxian formulation that "religion is an opiate..." is an apt observation when viewing youths in cults.

Within religious institutions criticism of modern established religious practice resonates, resulting in strategies for change, especially in Judaism. Rabbi James Rudin has offered a four-point program for the Jewish community to counteract cult attraction.[4] On the other hand, rabbis such as Richard Israel, Director of the Greater Boston Hillel Foundation, is typical of those who maintain that the loss of Jews to cults is of minor importance compared with the greater effects of intermarriage, anti-Semitism, drug abuse and the low level of current Jewish education. Rabbi Israel is among those who have not responded to the "cult alarm."

Kits of materials have been developed by various Jewish communal groups and parent organizations in many parts of the United States who *are* concerned, to inform families or individuals concerning cult behavior and the subtleties of their proselytizing. Some of these materials are listed in Section V.

The bibliography that follows attempts to guide readers to a variety of points of view on Jews and cults, in both popular and professional journals — with the largest proportion of citations indicated in Section IVa. As this topic is still in its developmental states, pamphlets, documents and miscellany are listed in Section VI, while a sampling of organizational literature by Jewish groups and others is listed in Section V. A reference section for further use of this Bibliography/Resource Guide is also provided.

Any *significant* omissions on *Jews and Cults* that predate the 1970s are regretted, and will be of interest to the writer if addressed to him, care of the publisher.

My thanks to Doris Gold in the preparation of this work, and to the research of Rabbi James Rudin and Marcia Rudin on the number of Jews in cults.

Jack Nusan Porter, Ph.D.
September 1981

Notes

1   Father James LeBar, representing the Roman Catholic Archdiocese of New York, offers these figures for estimates of Unification (Moonies) N.Y. membership: 45% from Catholic background; 40% from Protestant; and 10-12% from Jewish. Galen Kelly has found that 40% of his deprogrammed subjects were Protestant, 30% Catholic and 30% Jewish.

2   Reported in Anson D. Shupe, Jr., and David G. Bromley, "Witches, Moonies, and Accusations of Evil" in Thomas Robbins and Dick Anthony (eds.), *In Gods We Trust: New Patterns of Religious Pluralism in America*. Transaction Books, 1981, p. 253.

3   Reported in *Moment*, November 1978, by Michael Appell.

4   See Rudin an Rubin (1980) citattion in Section II, Background Reading: General Books

"Cults" — A Note on Definition

The bibliography that follows defines "cults," for purposes of inclusion, as:

> A rigid, often authoritarian,
> and esoteric religious sect
> that demands obsessive devo-
> tion to one leader or ideal.

It does not include materials on the *occult*, i.e., astro-
logical, magic, ESP, witchcraft, or sensitivity groups, nor
does it attempt to include current developments involving evangelical missionary groups (and their possible
relationships with Jews), though some citations about
them remain. Emphasis has been placed on "modern" or
"contemporary cults" or what sociologists have called "al-
ternate religions," "authoritarian sects," or "new religious
movements."

Black-Jewish sects (sometimes self-identified as "Israelites")[1] and their activities in the United States and in
Israel have also been included in Periodicals, Section IVb.

Notes

1   Those now residing in Israel.

RESOURCES

I. Bibliographies and Encyclopedias

Robbins, Thomas, comp. *Civil Liberties, "Brainwashing" and "Cults": A Selected Annotated Bibliography.* 2nd, revised/ expanded ed., Berkeley, Calif.: Center for the Study of New Religious Movements, Graduate Theological Union, January 1981, 48 pp. A very useful and objective bibliography with about 130 items on these specific themes. Recommended.

Task Force on Missionary Activity, "Selected Bibliography on Cults." Jewish Community Relations Council of New York, Inc., 1980.

Melton, J. Gordon. *Encyclopedia of American Religions.* Wilmington, N.C.: McGrath Publishing Co., 1979. This massive, two-volume, 1,203-page cross-referenced and indexed handbook is one of the most complete listings of American religions available today. It also includes descriptions of cults.

Encyclopedia Judaica. Jerusalem: Keter Publishing Company (Macmillan), 1972. (With supplementary yearbooks.) While somewhat weak on contemporary non-Jewish cults, it is a compendium of vast knowledge on Kabbalah Jewish sects and cults, Jewish magic, and religious movements. Should not be overlooked by readers.

II.   Background Reading: General Books

Baeck, Leo. *Judaism and Christianity*. New York: Atheneum, 1970.

Boettcher, Robert. *Gifts of Deceit*. New York: Holt, Rinehart & Winston, 1980. Boettcher was the staff director of the congressional subcommittee (the so-called "Fraser Committee") that investigated the activities of the "Moonies" organization in America and other parts of the world. An important work.

Boa, Kenneth. *Cults, World Religions, and You*. Wheaton, Ill.: Victor Books, 1977.

Bromley, David G., and Anson D. Shupe. *"Moonies" in America: Cult, Church and Crusade*. Beverly Hills, Calif.: Sage Publications, 1979. 272 pages. This book examines the Unification Church through a special sociological technique — the resource mobilization perspective, which emphasizes organizational rather than social-psychological aspects of a cult.

Buber, Martin. *Two Types of Faith*. New York: Harper & Row, 1961. This world-renowned theologian deals with the twin faiths of Christianity and Judaism.

Conway, Flo, and Jim Siegelman. *Snapping: America's Epidemic of Sudden Personality Change*. New York: J.B. Lippincott, 1978. As the title implies, this book is about a phenomenon in America called "snapping," and it covers not only cults, but also kidnapping (the Patricia Hearst case), quasi-psychological groups (like Silva Mind Control, est), and other forms of total thought reform and sudden personality changes based on such brainwashing. Controversial.

Cox, Harvey. *Turning East*. New York: Simon & Schuster, 1977. Professor Cox, a well-known theologian and religious activist, has written not a scholarly book but a personal odyssey through the world of Eastern religions. His presentation is fair but has been criticized for being too tolerant of certain groups such as the Krishnas. While there are useful treatments of many "cults," Jewish readers will find his chapter, "Meditation and Sabbath" especially enlightening, giving one a new, "Oriental" perspective on the role of the Shabbat in Jewish life.

Eastman, Roger. *The Ways of Religion.* San Francisco: Harper & Row (Canfield Press), 1975. A useful compendium of world religions, similar to the Needleman books listed here.

Enroth, Ronald. *Youth, Brainwashing, and the Extremist Cults.* Grand Rapids, Mich.: Zondervan Publishing House 1977. Written by a sociologist and a confirmed Christian, this book is nonetheless useful for Jewish parents who would like to find out more about specific cults such as the Moonies, the Krishnas, the Children of God, etc.

Gutman, Ernest. *The Hebrew-Christians.* Philadelphia: Dorrance, 1973. Discusses Jews and Christians who believe in Jesus Christ.

Horowitz, Irving Louis (ed.). *Science, Sin and Scholarship: The Politics of Reverend Moon and the Unification Church.* Cambridge, Mass.: M.I.T. Press, 1978. A collection of essays dealing with the "Moonies" and written by sociologists, journalists, and theologians. The Unification Church served the M.I.T. Press with a libel suit, but the courts dismissed the suit.

Jack, Alex (ed.). *The New Age Dictionary.* Brookline, Mass.: Kanthaka Press, 1976. Published by the East-West Foundation, this is a useful dictionary for any student and scholar who comes across unknown terms in the area of "new age" and cult knowledge. Strong in Hebrew and Jewish terms.

Kerns, Phil, with Doug Wead. *People's Temple, People's Tomb.* Plainfield, N.J.: Logos International, 1979. One of the quickie books put out after the Guyana tragedy, this one is written by a young man whose sister and mother were members of Jonestown. There were several Jews involved in the leadership of Jonestown.

Mathison, Richard. *Faiths, Cults, and Sects of America: From Atheism to Zen.* Indianapolis, Ind.: Bobbs-Merrill, 1960.

Matson, Katinka. *The Psychology Today Omnibook of Personal Development.* New York: William Morrow, 1977. An excellent and very useful guide to the quasi-cultic, quasi-therapeutic groups that exist in the counterculture from Arica to Esalen to Zen.

Needleman, Jacob, and George Baker (eds.). *Understanding the New Religions.* New York: The Seabury Press, 1978. A useful compendium of essays and articles on various religions that are "new" to the West. The senior author is a well-known professor of religions at San Francisco State University.

Needleman, Jacob, et al. (eds.). *Religion for a New Generation.* New York: Macmillan, 1973. A very fine anthology on the new Eastern, Oriental and neo-Western religions in North America, including Jewish sects.

Neubauer, Adolf, and S.R. Driver. *The Fifty-Third Chapter of Isaiah According to Jewish Interpreters.* New York: KTAV, 1969, two vols. This chapter in Isaiah is crucial in understanding the Jews for Jesus and similar groups because they quote this source as predicting the coming of a Messiah.

Robbins, Thomas, and Dick Anthony (eds.). *In Gods We Trust: New Patterns of Religious Pluralism in America.* New Brunswick, N.J.: Transaction Books, Inc., 1981. A collection of articles on why people join cults, the nature of conversion, and other sociological and theological issues. Many of these articles first appeared in the social science journal, *Society.* (Contains works by author of this bibliography.)

Rosten, Leo (ed.). *Religions of America.* New York: Simon & Schuster (Touchstone Books), 1975. A useful guidebook to the major American religions, from Jehovah's Witnesses to Black Baptists. With membership figures, charts, and social histories.

Rudavsky, David. *Modern Jewish Religious Movements.* New York: Behrman House, 1972. A basic text on modern Jewish religious movements, especially the many forms of Hasidism. Useful in understanding today's religious upsurge.

Rudin, A. James and Marcia R. Rudin. *Prison or Paradise: The New Religious Cults.* Philadelphia: Fortress Press, 1980. Written by the well-known Assistant National Director of Interreligious Affairs of the American Jewish Committee and his wife, this book, based on ten years of research, is valuable for both professionals and laypeople on the cult phenomenon.

Sklar, Dusty. *Gods and Beasts: The Nazis and the Occult.* New York: T.Y. Crowell, 1977. A controversial book that has provoked several cults because the author has dared to compare the early Nazis with cult behavior today.

Smith, Huston. *The Religions of Man.* New York: Harper & Row (Perennial Library), 1965. A good, concise paperback handbook on the major religions of the world, especially strong on Eastern religions.

Sontag, Frederick. *Sun Myung Moon and the Unification Church.* Nashville, Tenn.: Abingdon, 1977. This is an "in-depth" investigation of the man and the movement, but how in-depth is questionable. The publisher, in an unusual move, gives notice that it does not endorse Sontag's views. This book is a perfect example of how intelligent and scholarly men and women can be hoodwinked into believing almost anything and suppressing the negative through flattery, good food, money and respect. With these elements one can buy almost any intellectual, except for the rare few who are not brainwashed by these methods.

Sparks, Jack. *The Mindbenders: A Look at Current Cults.* Nashville, Tenn., and New York: Thomas Nelson, 1977. May turn some Jewish readers off by its highly evangelical Christian style and its overly dramatic interpretations. This book is anti-cult, but from a born-again fundamentalist position.

Spiritual Community Guide and *The New Consciousness Source Book SPG #4*. San Rafael, Calif.: Spiritual Community Publications, 1979. The best and possibly the most up-to-date sourcebook on cults, sects and "new" religions is the *Spiritual Community Guide*, as well as other materials from this organization. Very colorfully designed and highly recommended for libraries and researchers.

Steiner, Rudolf. *The Steinerbook Dictionary of the Psychic, Mystic, and Occult*. Blauvelt, N.Y.: Rudolf Steiner Publications, 1973. A cult has developed around this European mystic and psychic, but the dictionary is fascinating, off-beat and useful.

Stoner, Carol, and Jo Anne Burke. *All God's Children: The Cult Experience — Salvation or Slavery*. Philadelphia: Chilton Book Co., 1977. (Also available in Penguin paperback, 1979.) One of the better introductions to the world of cults. Based on interviews and case histories (including several Jewish families), this book is a wealth of fresh information. The authors try to be objective, which is difficult when discussing such an emotional topic. Highly recommended.

Talmon, Yonina. "Pursuit of the Millennium: The Relation Between Religion and Social Change," *Archives Européenes de Sociologie*, Vol. 1, 1962, pp. 125-148. A by-now classic study by an Israeli historian on the role of religion in transforming society.

III. Books: Jewish Views of Cults

Berger, David, and Michael Wyschograd. *Jews and Jewish Christianity*. New York: KTAV, 1978. Helpful in understanding "Jewish Christians" such as the Jews for Jesus, but also useful to any Jewish person who needs answers to the distorted claims that it is fine for a Jew to worship Jesus. Highly recommended.

Cohen, Daniel, *The New Believers: Young Religion in America.* New York: Ballantine, 1975. A short collection of descriptions of various cults, this book is geared for younger readers, junior and senior high school students, and it is quite good. Could be used in Hebrew schools.

Freed, Joshua. *Moonwebs.* Toronto, Ontario, Canada: Dorset Publishing Co., 1980. Another personal account of life in the Unification Church. The author is Jewish.

Friedlander, Gerald. *The Jewish Sources of the Sermon on the Mount.* New York: KTAV, revised ed., 1969.

Gonzalez-Wippler, Migene. *A Kabbalah for the Modern World.* New York: Bantam Books, 1977. (Orig. published by Julian Press, 1974.) I mention this book because Jewish mysticism has become so popular in America. Influenced by the works of Gershom Scholem, it has assumed almost cult-like proportions and in the process has become distorted in order to fit iconoclastic ends. This book, however, does give a factual overview of *Kabbalah* in an attempt to answer such questions as: What is the soul? What is the *female* role in the creation of the universe? Is the sex act divine or profane? And similar metaphysical questions.

Heifetz, Harold (ed.) *Zen and Hasidism.* Wheaton, Ill.: Quest Books, 1978. Heifetz, a novelist and playwright was intrigued by the similarities in the spiritual disciplines of Zen and Hasidism, especially the elements of joy, dependence on a guru *(rebbe)*, the influence of sayings (koans) and stories about the spiritual masters, etc. Out of his interest emerged this delightful collection of articles: a comparison of life in a *yeshiva* and a Zen monastery with articles by Meister Eckhart, Jiri Langer, John Blofeld, and Louis Ginzberg; the virtue of "sitting" by William Kramer, Christmas Humphreys, and Jacob Yuroh Teshima; and a lively debate on whether a Jew can practice Zen Buddhism and still remain a Jew, with Zalman Schachter and others. Highly recommended.

Levine, Edward M. "The Case for Deprogramming Religious Cult Members," *Society*. March/April, 1980. Special issue on Brainwashing. The author is a Jewish sociologist from Chicago, Illinois.

Levine, Faye. *The Strange World of the Hare Krishnas.* New York: Fawcett Publications, 1974. Written by a young Jewish woman, this is an insider's view of the Hare Krishna cult.

Levine, Samuel. *You Take Jesus, I'll Take God: How to Refute Christian Missionaries.* Los Angeles: Hamorah Press, 1980. This is a "complete guide" to dealing with Christian missionaries, showing the techniques they use to proselytize.

Lichtenstein, Morris. *Jewish Science and Health: A Textbook.* New York: Jewish Science Publications Corporation, 1955. 334 pp. Written by a rabbi, this book is the Jewish equivalent to a Christian Scientist text. It is also a unique and very small Jewish sect.

Patrick, Ted, and Tom Dulack. *Let Our Children Go!* New York: E.P. Dutton, 1976. The controversial California "deprogrammer" tells of his sometimes hair-raising experiences in cult rescue. A bit too hysterical and overly dramatic, the book does tend to gloss over the real legal and physical problems of kidnapping. But in some cases, it is the only alternative! Some of the examples deal with Jewish youth and their families.

Shupe, Anson, and David Bromley. *The New Vigilantes: The Anti-Cult Movement in America.* Beverly Hills, Calif.: Sage Publications, 1980. A new kind of book and approach: one that sees the *anti-cult* groups as the *problem* rather than the other way around. Interesting perspective on anti-cult groups, which often include Jews and Jewish groups in their membership.

Weiss-Rosmarin, Trude. *Judaism and Christianity: The Difference.* New York: Jonathan David, 1973. Important and useful for countering claims by Jewish or Christian missionaries regarding the true relationship between Judaism and Christianity.

Yanoff, Morris. *Where Is Joey? Lost Among the Hare Krishnas.* Athens, Ohio: Ohio University Press and Swallow Press 1981. An unusual book for a university press, but an interesting title nevertheless. It is a story that could easily be made into a movie, starring someone like Walter Matthau. Morris Yanoff's 12-year-old grandson Joe disappears into the Hare Krishna cult, and Yanoff, with his retired but very feisty friends, track down the young boy and return him to his family. This is obviously a Jewish family, and Morris Yanoff is a Brooklyn-born (1907) retired union organizer.

IVa   Selected Articles: *Jewish & General Views of Cults*

"Alternative Religions and the First Amendment," Special issue. *New York University Review of Law and Social Change*, 1981. Another look at the legal aspects of cults, here called "alternative religions" (more neutral language).

Adler, Rachel. "The Concept of Messiah in Jewish Tradition," *Davka*, Vol. II, No. 2, March-April 1972, pp. 2-6. The lead article in a special issue on Jesus and the Jews. Adler examines the different meanings attached to the concept of Messiah in both Christianity and Judaism.

Andron, Sandy. "Our Gifted Teens and the Cults," *Pedagogic Reporter*, Vol. 31, Fall 1979, pp. 37-38. She states that 12-15 percent of the cult population is Jewish and most are "gifted" young people. She explains why this is so and what can be dome about it.

Anon. "The Man Who Bends Science." *And It Is Divine*, Vol. 1 Issue 7, May 1973, pp. 38 cf. A feature about Israeli psychic Uri Geller in the official journal of the Divine Light Mission. Who is using whom?

Appell, Michael. "Cult Encounters, *Moment*, Vol. 4, No. 1, November 1978, pp. 19-24. A short, well-written essay on the cult dilemma. Based on interviews with parents who have a child in a cult as well as with various Jewish professionals involved in cults.

Birnholtz, R.J. "Jewish Assertiveness in Combating Missionaries," *Jewish Digest*, vol. 24, November 1978, pp. 18-23.

Black, David. "The Secrets of the Innocents: Why Kids Join Cults," *Women's Day*, February 1977, pp. 91 cf. An article on the cult phenomenon in a popular national magazine, which evoked an important response on the public's part. My colleague's name (Prof. Irvin Doress) and address were mentioned, and he received so many letters he contacted me to join him in writing a booklet on the subject (*Kids in Cults*).

"Brainwashing," special issue of *Society*, Vol. 17, No. 3, March-April 1980, pp. 19-50. A special issue devoted to whether cults actually "brainwash" their victims. The contributors are mainly sociologists.

Brickner, Balfour. "Christian Missionaries and a Jewish Response," *Worldview*, Vol. 1, No. 5, 1978. Reprinted in *Jewish Digest*, Summer 1978, pp. 10-19. Why Christians should not try to convert Jews.

Brickner, Balfour. "America's Religion: What's Right, What's Left," *Present Tense*, Vol. 8, No. 3, Spring 1981, pp. 40-43. A forceful, liberal critique of the new politicized "Moral Majority," its legion of Christian evangelicals, and their threat to both liberal and Jewish values.

Edelstein, Andrew. "Cults Are Rising as Social Peril," *Jewish Week*, April 12, 1981, p. 52. A description of a two-day conference on cults sponsored by the Jewish Community Relations Council of New York and the Jewish Board of Family and Children's Services. All agreed that, despite less media coverage, cults continued to pose a problem. Increase education, information, and more support systems were put forth as partial solutions to the problem.

Bromley, David G., and Anson D. Shupe, Jr. "Financing the New Religions: A Resource Mobilization Approach,"

Journal for the Scientific Study of Religion, Vol. 19, No. 3, September 1980, pp. 227-239. Two sociologists explore how the cults raise so much money by examining the "organizational infrastructure" of such fund-raising strategies.

Bruning, Fred. "Europe's Rising Cults," *Newsweek* (Religion section), Ma 7, 1979, pp. 100-102. A description of cult movements in Europe where they are also fairly popular, especially Scientology, Children of God (also called the Family of Love), and the Unification Church.

Bush, Larry. "The Challenge of the Cults," *Jewish Currents*, December 1980, pp. 9-13, cf. A very well written progressive analysis of the cult phenomenon.

Cohen, Mark. "Missionaries in our Midst: The Appeal of Alternatives," *Analysis*, March 1978, No. 64, 8 pp. A report on cults and Hebrew-Christians. It is especially strong on missionary groups to the Jews.

Cohen, Robert A. "Infiltrating the Jews for Jesus," *St. Louis Jewish Light*, Vol. 33, No. 25, 1978. Reprinted in *Jewish Digest*, February 1979, pp. 8-12. The story of Rabbi Moishe Greenwald, Midwest regional director of the National Conference of Synagogue Youth, an Orthodox youth movement, and his deliberate initiation into a local Jews for Jesus group in St. Louis.

"Confronting the Moonies," *United Synagogue Review Quarterly*, Vol. 30, Summer 1977, p. 3.

Coser, Rose, and Lewis Coser. "Jonestown as Perverse Utopia," *Dissent*, Spring 1979, pp. 158-163. Should be read in conjunction with Midge Decter's analysis of Jonestown. (This article is more revealing.)

"Cults Pose Challenge to Parents, Jewish Community," *Women's World* (B'nai B'rith Women), February/March 1981, p. 6. A short overview of the problems posed by the cults. There is also a personal account of the deprogramming of a young member of the Divine Light Mission with the help of Ted Patrick, written by a B'nai B'rith woman member.

Davis, Maurice. "Moon — For the Misbegotten," *Reform Judaism*, November 1974. A powerful indictment of the Unification Church written by one of the most eloquent anti-cult spokespersons.

Davis, Rabbi Maurice. "Update on Moon," *Brotherhood*, March-April 1977.

Decter, Midge. "The Politics of Jonestown," *Commentary*, May 1979, pp. 29-34. A strongly written article, in the *Commentary* vein of redbaiting, that sees the People's Temple of Rev. Jim Jones as a natural outgrowth of 1960s radicalism. She makes a good case, but her hysterical tone and over-generalization provide no real insight into the general cult phenomenon, though it might explain the Jonestown cult in terms of revolutionary suicide. In the end, however, Decter merely uses this bizarre case as a weapon to bludgeon the entire political left in the United States.

Delgado, Richard. "Religious Totalism," *Southern California Law Review*, Vol. 51, No. 1, November 1977, pp. 1-98. Practically the entire issue of this law journal is taken up by Delgado's legal analysis — that the state and parents have a right to intervene if a child is threatened with physical or mental abuse.

Delgado, Richard. "Investigating Cults," *The New York Times*, Op-Ed page, Wednesday, December 27, 1978. Delgado questions the idea that the state or private groups can never intervene into cult activity.

Doress, Irvin, and Jack Nusan Porter. "Kids in Cults," *Society*, Vol. 15, No. 4, May-June 1978, pp. 69-71. An abridged version of the Doress-Porter pamphlet listed. This version is reprinted in Thomas Robbins and Dick Anthony (eds.), *In Gods We Trust*, New Brunswick, N.J.: Transaction Books, 1981.

Dworkin, Susan. "Jews who Seek Eastern Mysticism," *Hadassah Magazine*, May 1974. Reprinted in *Jewish Digest*, January 1975, pp. 9-14.

Editorial. "The Fruits of Fanaticism," *Reconstructionist*, Vol. 44, January 1979, pp. 3-4.

Eichhorn, D.M. "Hebrew Christianity," *Jewish Spectator*, Vol. 41, Fall 1976, pp. 33-35.

Enroth, Ronald M. "Any Preventive for the Cults?" *Christian Herald*, Vol. 102, No. 3, March 1979, pp. 13-15. Enroth is a sociologist and religious leader, and his views coincide with many Jewish professionals on the subject.

Freedman, Theodore. "Religious Cults: How Serious a Danger?" *ADL Bulletin*, Vol. 34, April 1977, pp. 1-2.

Furstenberg, Rochelle. "From Gurus to Gemara: Women Return to Tradition," *Hadassah Magazine*, Vol. 59, January 1978, pp. 14-15 cf. The story of young Jewish women who move from Eastern religions to traditional, orthodox Judaism.

Gittelsohn, Roland B. "Jews for Jesus: Are They Real?" *Midstream*, Vol. 25, May 1979, pp. 41-45.

Goldberg, W. et al. "Deprogramming: An Exchange," *American Zionist*, Vol. 68, October 1977, pp. 34-38.

Haramgaal, Y. "Deprogramming: A Critical View," *American Zionist*, Vol. 67, May-June 1977, pp. 16-19.

Harder, M. "Sex Roles in the Jesus Movement," *Social Compass*, Vol. 21, 1974, pp. 345-353.

Hilburn, Robert. "The Gospel According to Bob," *Boston Globe*, Wednesday, November 26, 1980, Living Section, p. 27. This is an interview with Bob Dylan, the famous troubadour of music and mystical politics and why he, a young Jewish man, became a born-again Christian. As Dylan puts it: "This is no maharishi trip with me. Jesus is definitely not that to me... Most of the people I know don't believe that Jesus was resurrected, that He is alive..."

Hurvitz, Mark, and Aron Manheimer (eds.). "Jesus?" A special issue of *Davka*, Vol. II, No. 2, March-April 1972, 64 pages. *Davka*, a Los Angeles Jewish countercultural journal that recently folded to our great loss, was one of the first Jewish journals to see the impact of cults and, especially, the ambivalent relationship that Jews have with Jesus.

Israel, Richard J. "The Cult Problem Is a Fake!" in the "Headlines and Footnotes" section, *the National Jewish Monthly*, January 1980. This provocative "Op-Ed" piece states that (a) there are about a million students in Boston; (b) of these there are 38,000 Jewish students; (c) of the 70 Hare Krishna people there, half are Jewish; (d) of the other cults, their Jewish proportion is even less; and (e) we probably lose more than 35 young Jews to suicide every year than we lose to the Hare Krishnas! Israel, the director of the Greater Boston Hillel Foundations, is in a position to know the Jewish population better than most of us, and he may very well be right. The cults are a problem but *not* the most important one facing the Jewish people.

Jacobs, Steven. "How to Answer the Christian Missionary," *Jewish Digest*, September 1975, pp. 14-17.

Jacobs, Steven. "Are Your Children Immune from Missionaries?" *Jewish Digest*, Vol. 23, December 1977, pp. 10-12. Originally appeared in *Brotherhood* (National Federation of Temple Brotherhood, Reform Judaism), Vo. 11, No. 1, 1977.

Jahnke, Art. "They Call Him the Negative Messiah, *Real Paper* (Boston), August 28, 1980, p. 7. A fascinating interview with Steve Hassan, founder and president of Ex-Moon, an organization composed of former members of the Unification Church and dedicated to exposing the deceit and scandal they claim permeates the church. Steve Hassan is a young Jewish man from the New York area who rose to the rank of assistant to the director of the church's national headquarters in New York City.

Jewish Week, "Cults Said to Have Entrapped 1,000 Jewish Kids in this Area," April 12, 1981, p. 32. A report by Malcolm Hoenlein of the New York Jewish Community Relations Council, who estimated that over 1,000 Jewish young people were involved in cults and that 60 different missionary groups which control 1,700 radio and 100 TV stations reaching more than 1.5 million people very week are active in the New York area. These figures, of course, comprise evangelical Christian missionaries more so than cults like the Moonies and Krishnas, who to my knowledge have limited access to mass radio and TV.

Kaslow, Florence, and Marvin B. Sussman. "Cults and the Family," *Marriage and Family Review*, Fall 1981. A special issue entirely devoted to the cult's impact on the family with contributions by noted social workers and others. Especially pertinent to Jewish families as well.

Kollin, Gilbert. "The Call of the Strange Cults," *Jewish Digest*, October 1980, pp. 25-32. Originally appeared in the *Reconstructionist*, Vol. 45, No. 10, 1980. A liberal, religious interpretation of why young Jews choose other religions — affluence, spiritual poverty, permissiveness. A piece both serious and humorous. To Kollin, cults are a warning bell that the "process of assimilation has passed the danger point."

LeMoult, John E. "De-programming Members of Religious Sects," *Fordham Law Review*, March 1978, pp. 599-640. Should be juxtaposed with the Richard Delgado legal article since the author points out several abuses that can take place, especially abuses of First Amendment rights. This tricky question of kidnapping and deprogramming needs to be carefully explored.

Lester, Elenore. "Cultists Focusing on Young Jews as Prime Prospects," *Jewish Week*, December 28-January 4, 1981. A discussion of the response of the New York Jewish community to the "strong increase in missionary and cult activity during the past few years."

Levy, Richard. "Passion and Passivity: Three Musical Crucifictions," *Davka*, Vol. II, No. 2, March-April 1972, pp. 35-41. Written by a Hillel rabbi from UCLA, this analysis addresses the subtle gospel of *Jesus Christ Superstar,*

Godspell, and Leonard Bernstein's *Mass* as "cruci-fictions" (note the beautiful pun here) of Jewish history as a tool for proselytizing, and by Jews no less, doing the missionizing through the popular media.

Livneh, Eliezer. "Judaism and the Religions of the Far East," *Judaism*, 1951.

Luxenberg, Stan. "The Soul Snatchers of Long Island," *Moment*, Vol. 2, May 1977, pp. 7-10. The fight against Jews for Jesus forcefully told.

Malamed, Gad. "How to Answer Street Missionaries," *Jewish Digest*, Vol. 22, February 1977, pp. 49-51. (Originally appeared in *Kol Yavneh*, Vol. 4, No. 5, 1976.)

Mitchell, Elicahi, and Shira Lindsay. "Jews Do Believe in Jesus," *Davka*, Vol. II, No. 2, March-April 1972, pp. 7-17. Written by two Jews for Jesus, possibly converts to Judaism, this is a rare analysis of Jesus and Judaism from such a perspective.

Neff, Carol. "B'nai B'rith Confronts the Cults," *National Jewish Monthly*, Vol. 94, November 1979, pp. 23-25.

Pearlstein, Ira. "The Reverend Moon Phenomenon," *Jewish Student Press Service*, 1976. (Reprinted in *Jewish Digest*, June 1976, pp. 55-59.)

Pearlstein, Ira. "Jews and Reverend Moon," *Women's American ORT Reporter*, March-April 1977, pp. 3 cf. Pearlstein states in his first paragraph that one-third of the Moonies are Jewish, which would be anywhere from 3,000-10,000 Jews. I think those figures are very high. No one really knows, but Jews do play a prominent role in the Unification Church. While superficial, the article is useful and should be read along with David Silverberg's piece in *Present Tense* (Autumn 1976).

Porter, Jack Nusan. "Confronting the Media: The Impact of Jonestown on One Sociologist," *The New England Sociologist*, Vol. 1, No. 2, Spring/Summer 1979, pp. 84-88. How one sociologist confronted the media in the wake of the Jonestown massacre, his experiences with television, radio and newspaper interviewers, etc.

Porter, Jack Nusan. "Many Jewish Professors at Moon's Conference in Boston," *The Jewish Advocate*, December 1, 1978. A journalistic account on the 7th International Conference on the Unity of the Sciences sponsored by the Unification Church, showing how many Jewish and Israeli professors and scholars were in attendance and why.

Porter, Jack Nusan. "Religious Cults/Religious Fascism," *Jewish Currents* (forthcoming). Porter discusses the Jewish component in cults, especially the number of Jewish scholars who were tricked into attending Reverend Moon's conferences, scholars like R.J. Zwi Werblowsky, Oscar Handlin, and Richard Rubenstein. Also mentions the anti-progressive politics of most cults.

Raab, Earl. "Reverend Moon and the Jews: The San Francisco Experience," *Congress Monthly* Vol. 43, December 1976, pp. 8-12.

Rabinove, Samuel. "Legal Encounters of a Religious Kind," *Keeping Posted*, February 1978, pp. 3-7. Deals with legal problems of church-state relations. (Other articles on the same topic in the above issue.)

Rachleff, Owen. "The Jewish Occultniks," *Midstream*, Vol. 22, No. 1, 1976. (Also appeared in *Jewish Digest*, September 1976, pp. 22-26.) Describes the trend of the Jewish occult and esoterics among world Jewry, often in novel and sophisticated ways.

Rausch, David A. "American Evangelicals and the Jew," *Midstream*, February 1977.

Rausch, David A. "Evangelical Zionism: The Vicious Debate Among Evangelicals," *Jewish Frontier*, May 1977, pp. 28-30.

Rausch, David A. "Jews Evangelized: Messianic Jews," *Midstream*, Vol. 25, May 1979, pp. 36-41.

Rice, Berkeley. "Messiah from Korea: Honor Thy Father Moon," *Psychology Today*, January 1976, pp. 36-45 cf. One of the early articles in mass media publications on the Unification church by a Jewish writer.

Robbins, Thomas. "Deprogramming the 'Brainwashed': Even a Moonie Has Civil Rights," *The Nation*, February 26, 1977, pp. 238-242. A plea for civil liberties regarding people in cults. The author, who is Jewish, criticizes both the concept and the act of "deprogramming" and "brainwashing."

Robbins, Thomas. "Cults and the Therapeutic State," *Social Policy Magazine*, May/June 1979. Robbins is against intervention as an attack against individual freedom and religious liberty.

Robbins, Thomas, and Dick Anthony. "Harassing Cults," *The New York Times*, Op-Ed Page, Thursday, October 16, 1980. Discusses the "bias against foreign sects promoting strange gods and gurus" and concludes that religious freedom must also apply to groups that are unorthodox and even bizarre.

Robbins, Thomas. "Religious Movements, The State and the Law: Reconceptualizing 'The Cult Problem,'" *New York University Review of Law and Social Change*, Vol. IX, No. 1, 190-1981, pp. 33-49. Another contribution by a well-known authority on religious groups. Robbins emphasizes that wile there are social and legal problems posed by some of these highly authoritarian communal movements, it is "mystifying and inimical" to civil liberties to label the problem as essentially one of "brainwashing and mind control." He cautions whether the state should intervene in these issues.

Rudi James, and Marcia R. Rudin. "Onward (Hebrew) Christian Soldiers," *Present Tense*, Vol. 4, No. 4, Summer 1977, pp. 17-26. An in-depth report on the Hebrew-Christians (also known as Messianic Jews) in the New York area.

Rudin, A. James. "The Peril of Reverend Moon," *Jewish Digest*, vol. 22, June 1977, pp. 74-78.

Rudin, Marcia R. "The New Religious Cults and the Jewish Community," Symposium on Religious Education and Spiritual Quest. *Religious Education*, vol. 73, May-June 1978, pp. 350-360.

Schachter, Zalman. "Toward an Order of B'nai Or," *Judaism*, Spring 1964. A well-known *Jewish* guru presents his views on religious *communitas*.

Schulweiss, Harold M. "The Public and Private Agenda in Jewish Education," *Pedagogic Reporter*, Vol. 30, Fall 1978, pp. 2-6.

Schulweiss, Harold M. "The Challenge of the New Secular Religions," *Conservative Judaism*, Vol. 32, Summer 1979, pp. 3-15.

Schwartz, Lita Linzer. "A Note on Family Rights, Cults and the Law," *Journal of Jewish Communal Service*, Vol. 55, Summer 1978, pp. 194-198.

Schwartz, Lita Linzer. "Cults and the Vulnerability of Jewish Youth," *Jewish Education*, Summer 1978, pp. 23-26 cf.

Schwartz, Lita Linzer, and Florence Kaslow. "Cults, the Individual, and the Family," *Journal of Marital and Family Counseling*, April 1979.

Shanker, Thom. "New Cults — Why Now?" *ADL Bulletin*, vol. 36, Nos. 2 & 3, March-April 1979, pp. 13-14. The description of a conference on the cults sponsored by the ADL and attended by sociologists Marvin Bressler and Charles Glock and theologian Harvey Cox, among others.

Silver, Marc, and Barbara Pash. "Cults," *Baltimore Jewish Times*, June 3, 1977. An interesting article on the phenomenon based on actual research and interviews. This article was part of a series on the subject; other on June 17, 1977.

Silverberg, David. "Heavenly Deception: Reverend Moon's Hard Sell," *Present Tense*, Vol. 4, No. 1, Autumn 1976, pp.

49-56. This is a well-written and informative article on the Jewish element in the Unification Church, but it probes even deeper: what "turns off" young Jews about the Jewish "establishment" so that they join cults. Silverberg has some good quotes from Rabbi Maurice Davis and from a young Israeli "Moonie." He also briefly describes some major Jewish "Moonies" who are leaders in the church: Dr. Mose Hurst, who was cultural chairman of Hillel at the University of Oregon in the early 1960s; Dr. William Leslie Bergman, a medical doctor, who headed the Los Angeles branch and is now in New York City; and Dan Feffernan, secretary-general of the Freedom Leadership Foundation, who in 1976 founded another Moonie front called Judaism in Service to the World, which operated for a short time and then faded away. Highly recommended.

Singer, Margaret T. "In Search of Self: The Cult Culture," *Israel Horizons*, Vol. 27, No. 6, June 1979, pp. 18-21. A very useful article based on the author's research with ex-cult members. It deals with such issues as what characterizes the cults from other religions and what major problems, both psychological and social, ex-cultists face when leaving the cult world.

Singer, Margaret Thaler. "Coming Out of the Cults," *Psychology Today*, January 1979.

Solender, Elsa. "The Making and Unmaking of a Jewish Moonie," *National Jewish Monthly*, Vol. 93, December 1978. (Reprinted in *Jewish Digest*, Vol. 24, April 1979, pp. 18-24.)

Spero, Moshe Halevi. "Cults: Some Theoretical and Practical Perspectives," *Journal of Jewish Communal Service*, Vol. 53, No. 4, Summer 1977, pp. 330-338. A well-written and documented article by a young Jewish social worker showing how the cults cater to psychosocial and "cosmic" needs of modern adolescents. Highly recommended.

Sweet, Larry. "Why I Left the Moonies," *Jewish Digest*, Vol. 23, September 1977, pp. 67-70. A personal account that verifies many other observations of the group.

Swope, George W. "Kids and Cults," *Media and Methods,* May/June 1980, pp. 18-21, 49. The author is well known in the anti-cult area, his own child having been in one. He is also a psychologist and sociologist. This article, geared to teachers in high schools and colleges, is short but quite informative, especially his six-point system of what sort of person is vulnerable to the cults: idealistic, innocent, inquisitive, independent, identity seeking, and insecure. What is shocking is that these categories can describe almost any young person; thus, he maintains, that almost any young adult can be recruited given the proper circumstances.

Tabak, Lawrence. "Maharishi U — Learning to Levitate in Fairfield, Iowa," *Moment,* Vol. 4, No. 3, January-February 1979, pp. 26-32. A journalistic account of the presence of Jews in the TM movement, the meditation cult of His Holiness Maharishi Mahesh Yogi. Tabak concludes that nothing the Maharishi preaches is explicitly at odds with Judaism but the idea of total dependence on one master-teacher and the suspension of critical judgment is radically at odds with the Jewish way of life.

"The Issue Is Conversion," *Moment,* Vol. 4, No. 4, March 1979 pp. 17-35. A turnabout perspective. Joining a cult often entails conversion. But a controversy arose when Rabbi Alexander Schindler, president of the Union of American Hebrew Congregations, suggested that Jews actively launch a national crusade to welcome converts to Judaism. Contains Rabbi Schindler's statement and remarks by several other rabbis plus a rare set of interviews with Christians who have converted to Judaism. See also *Moment,* April 1977, vol. 2, pp. 34-38, for reader response to this issue.

Warsaw, Robin. "Anybody's Kid: Cults and the Jewish Connection," *Expo Magazine,* Spring 1979.

"The Uneasy Boundary: Church and State," Special Issue. *The Annals of the American Academy of Political and Social*

Science, Vol. 446, November 1979. Contains articles dealing with the social and legal aspects of cults.

Urofsky, M.I. "Does Jesus Make You Kosher?" *Jewish Observer*, Vol. 26, September 1, 1977. Deals with the Hebrew-Christian movement.

Wax, Judith. "Sharing a Son with Hare Krishna," *The New York Times Magazine*, May 1, 1977, pp. 40 cf. A Jewish mother tells her sad story of how her son became a Hare Krishna devotee.

Weber, Bill. "Jonestown Deaths May Spark Fight Against Cults," *The Lowell Sun*, November 26, 1978, p. C5. An example of the many articles on what the Jonestown killings/suicides mean to other cults in America.

Weiss-Rosmarin, Trude. "Did Jesus Fulfill the Hebrew Messianic Promises?" *Jewish Spectator*, Vol. 42, No. 4, Winter 1977, pp. 3-7. A dialogue between "Jeff," a searching young Jewish man, not a missionary, and the editor, Dr. Weiss-Rosmarin, on "proof" that the prophecies of the Israelite prophets were not fulfilled by Jesus Christ.

Weiss-Rosmarin, Trude. "The Most Dangerous Cult," *Jewish Spectator*, Vol. 44, Summer 1979, pp. 4-5.

Weizenbaum, Joseph. "Religion or Cult: Where Is the Line?" *Sh'ma*, March 1979.

"Yeshua Is the Messiah," *Time*, July 4, 1977. An article in the Religion section of the national newsmagazine depicting the growth of the Jews for Jesus.

Zakim, Leonard P. "Cults: A Calm Perspective," *The Jewish Advocate*, Thursday, July 5, 1979, p. 19. Written by a lawyer and the ADL civil rights director in Boston, this article tries to be objective about the cults. Zakim says we must take a balanced approach: counteracting them at the same time that civil and religious liberties are also observed.

Zeldner, Max. "Are We Losing Our Children?" *Jewish Frontier*, Vol. 44, May 1977, pp. 8-11. Another personal account of a friend who entered a cult.

IVb Black Jews[1]

Ben Yehuda, Shalaek. *Black Hebrew Israelites from America to the Promised Land: The Great International Religious Conspiracy Against the Children of the Prophets.* New York: Vantage Press, 1975. The personal story of one such Black Jewish leader from Chicago, Illinois.

Berger, Graenum. *Black Jews in America: A Documentary with Commentary.* New York: Commission on Synagogue Relations, Federation of Jewish Philanthropies, 1978. A useful historical account, with contemporary interpretations, of Black Jews. They are both a cult within American religious groups and a distinct type of Jew. Their Jewish aspects are discussed.

Brotz, Howard M. *The Black Jews of Harlem.* New York: Schocken Books, 1964. Though in need of updating, this book is among the few based on empirical observation of Black Jews.

Eder, Richard. "Black 'Israelites' Challenging Israel's Policies," *The New York Times*, August 31, 1971.

Ehrman, Albert. "Explorations and Responses: black Judaism in New York," *Journal of Ecumenical Studies*, Vol. 8, Winter 1971, pp. 103-114.

Korn, Shulamit. "Dimona: A Back Misunderstanding," *Jerusalem Post*, October 15, 1971. A discussion of the troubles Black Jewish cult members have had in Israel.

Landes, Ruth. "Nero Jews in Harlem," *Jewish Journal of Sociology*, Vol. 9, December 1967, pp. 175-188. A 1933 paper, destroyed by the Nazis, found and subsequently published. The author thought that this Black cult would eventually fail, yet it has remained a strong, viable group to this day.

Lavender, Abraham D. (ed.). "Black Jews" in his *A Coat of Many Colors: Jewish Subcommunities in the United States.* Westport, Conn.: Greenwood Press, 1977, pp. 209-232. A selection of articles on Black Jews with excellent references sections.

Lewin, James. "Back Hebrews Reconsidered," *The Jewish Advocate*, July 16, 1981, p. 15. A summary of the Black Hebrews in Israel, and some dilemmas about their status.

Manheimer, Aron. "The Black Israelites of Dimona," Parts I and II, *Davka*, Vol. II, No. 3, May/June 1972, pp. 6-12, 48-53. A good report on the sect of Black Jews known as Black Israelites and their problems setting in Israel.

Polner, Murray. "Being Black and Jewish," *National Jewish Monthly*, Vol. 87, October 1972, pp. 39-43.

Watzkin, Howard. "Black Judaism in New York," *Harvard Journal of Negro Affairs*, Vol. I, 1967, pp. 12-18.

Weisbord, Robert S. "Black Hebrew Israelites," *Judaism*, Vol. 24, No. 1, Winter 1975, pp. 23-38.

Windsor, Rudolph R. *From Babylon to Timbuktu*. Jericho, N.Y.: Exposition Press, 1969. An attempt to establish, through a historical view, the authenticity of Black Hebrews. (The author acknowledges his consultation with rabbis and Jewish sources.)

V. *Organizational Literature on Cults*[2]

American Family Foundation, Lexington, Mass.: *The Advisor.* A very useful and informative newspaper published by an anti-cult group, founded in 1979. Geared especially to politicians, lawyers and students.

American Jewish Committee, New York: Rudin, James, "Jews and Judaism in Reverend Moon's Divine Principle: A Report," December 1976. This report attempts to show how the Moon theology is anti-Semitic in some ways and how it places special burdens on Jews, a special indemnity for rejecting Christ.

American Jewish Congress, New York: Stern, Marc D. "The Cults and the Law," CLSA/UA Reports, Bulletin No. I, February 2, 1978. A report, written like a lawyer's brief, on various legislation and decisions regarding the cults. Very useful in any action taken against cult members.

Anti-Missionary Institute, New York: Morgan, Hesh. "Is This the End of the Battle?" 1979. AMI is a group in New York City that actively battles against cults and missionaries to the Jews, a kind of JDL religious task force. This handout plus other material is available from them.

Beth Sar Shalom, Englewood Cliffs, N.J.: "Not All Jews Are for Jesus," n.d. A nicely designed testimonial booklet about Jews in the Jews for Jesus movement telling why and how they joined. But note: this material was prepared by the Jews for Jesus themselves (in this case called Sar Shalom, Prince of Peace, meaning Jesus Christ, but using Hebrew terms).

B'nai B'rith/Hillel Foundations, Washington, D.C.: Fishman, Samuel Z. (ed.). *Jewish Students and the Jesus Movement*, 1973, paperback. A useful booklet on the Jesus Movement in the USA and Canada. Compiled by a Hillel Foundation officer, it is geared for students and young people and those working with such age groups.

B'nai B'rith/Hillel Foundations, Washington, D.C.: Fishman, Samuel Z. *Comments on the Campus: The Moonies and the Response of the Jewish Community*, 1977.

Board of Jewish Education, Baltimore: *The Cult Phenomenon*, 1978.

Hadassah, New York: Bay me, Steven. *Jewish Education Guide* (section on "Cults, Missionaries, and Jews for Jesus"), October 31, 1979, pp. 20-28. A useful discussion guide for Hadassah members. Also contains a short bibliography and suggestions for programs.

Hineni, Inc., Woodmere, N.Y.: *Hineni News*, a newsletter with photos. Rebbetzin, Esther Jungreis, president.

International Society for Krishna Consciousness, Los Angeles: *A Request to the Media: Please Don't Lump Us In*, 1979. A small booklet, published after the infamous Jonestown suicides, attempting, rather successfully, to show the media that there is a difference between other cults and the

Krishna variety. How successful they were in making a difference, again I am not sure, but it is a useful little pamphlet.

Jewish Community Relations Council, Philadelphia: *The Challenge of the Cults*, 1978, 70 pages. One of the best handbooks on cults and what to do about them. Every Jewish library interested in cults should have this volume.

Jewish Community Information Council, Lawrence, N.Y.: Dobin, Rabbi Rubin R. *Jews for Jews*. A kit of material edited and assembled by Rabbi Dobin for students, parents and educators.

Jews for Jews, Miami Beach, Fla.: Dobin, Rabbi Rubin R. *Watch Out! The Cults Will Trap You*. The material in this brochure was assembled from Rabbi Dobin's testimony before the New York Legislature about his experience in the Miami area. Rabbi Dobin also has other information kits on T.M., "Guru Hindu Cults," and other groups.

National Conference of Christians and Jews, New York: Perrin, Ann. "Cults: What Are They, and Is Governmental Intervention Warranted?" *The Dialogue*, March 1979, 6 pages. A pamphlet put out by the National Conference of Christians and Jews which questions governmental intrusion and legal intervention except in extreme cases. Suggests other methods of combating the cults.

National Conference of Synagogue Youth/NCSY and Union of Orthodox Jewish Congregations of America, New York: Kaplan, Aryeh and Associates. *The Real Messiah*, May 1976. A pamphlet distributed by the Orthodox Union with essays on Jews and Christians. Jesus from a Jewish point-of-view, and the Jewish view of the Messiah. Strongly recommended.

Jewish Community Relations Council of New York: "Task Force on Missionary Activity Update," The Missionaries Summer Campaign, 1977. A periodic report on information and developments in the missionary activity aimed at Jews in the New York Metropolitan area.

Jewish Community Relations Council of New York: *Resource Kit on Missionaries and Cults*, 1979.

Jews for Jesus, San Rafael, Calif.: Rosen, Moishe. "How to Witness Simply and Effectively to the Jews," n.d. A rare document written by one of the leaders of the Jews for Jesus on how to "witness" to Jews: what kind of Jew to go after, what to say, what *not* to say, what Biblical verses to quote, etc. A fascinating and hard-to-get document.

Syracuse Jewish Federation, Syracuse, N.Y.: "The Unification Church." Special issue of *The Jewish Connection*, 1977. Another attempt by a local Jewish community relations council to gather information on cults. This is a ragged, superficial compilation of material and too overblown to be useful. Compare it to the Philadelphia Jewish Community Relations Council booklet mentioned earlier and see the difference in quality.

Union of American Hebrew Congregations, New York: "Close Encounters: Church and State," *Keeping Posted*, Vol. 23, No. 5, February 1978, Special issue. An entire issue devoted to the relationship between church and state, of religious liberty, in America.

Union of American Hebrew Congregations, New York: *Missionary and Cult Movements*, 1979. A study guide.

United Synagogue of America, New York: *The Missionary at the Door*, 1972. A study guide.

VI   Miscellany (Documents, Addresses, etc.)

Davis, Rabbi Maurice. "Moon" address. Delivered at the Special Conference on Jewish Young Adults, Roslyn Heights, N.Y., November 9, 1975. See also *The Jewish Spectator*, 1976 issue.

Doress, Irvin, and Jack Nusan Porter. *Kids in Cults: Why They Leave*, Brookline, Mass.: Reconciliation (RC) Associates, 3rd edition, 1980. A pamphlet that succinctly answers the questions raised in the title. For parents, teachers, and students. Contains large bibliography and sources section. The senior author is a Boston psychotherapist whose daughter has been in the Hare Krishna movement for over eight years, but has recently left of her own volition.

Freedman, Theodore. "Evangelical Survey Findings," unpublished manuscript. New York: Anti-Defamation League of B'nai B'rith, 1977.

Cults and the Law, Symposium: American Jewish Congress, Thursday, December 13, 1979. Co-sponsored by the ADL and the American Jewish Committee.

Boettcher, Robert, K.H. Barney, Allen Tate Wood, and Steve Hassan. Statements given to the press, opposing the 7th International Conference on the Unity of the Sciences. Boston, Mass.: November 22, 1978. The conference is a "Moonie" front group.

Committee on International Relations, "The Moon Organization" in a report of the Subcommittee on International Organizations, Investigation of Korean-American Relations, Washington, D.C.: U.S. Government Printing Office, October 31, 1978, pp. 311-392. This famous document is an intensive investigation of the Unification Church, its leader, and "front" organizations. Highly recommended.

Hebrew Christian Pamphlets. "I Found the Messiah"; Dear Rabbi..."; "Jewishness and Hebrew Christianity" and others. Orangeburg, N.Y.: Beth Sar Shalom. A series of pamphlets used in missionary work by Hebrew Christians for the Jewish community. Such missions to the Jews go back many years (a century or more) before the present-day Jews for Jesus. Their point is that it is possible to be both a Jew and a believer in the messiahship of Jesus Christ.

"Horowitz Book: Smokescreen for Religious Persecution," statement distributed by the Boston Unification Church at the Boston Book Festival, Fall 1979. I.L. Horowitz had just edited a book called *Science, Sin and Scholarship: The Politics of Reverend Moon and the Unification Church* (M.I.T. Press). The Moonies felt the book was anti-Unification Church. They later sued the publishers for religious libel.

Juster, Daniel C. *Jewishness and Jesus*. Downers Grover, Ill.: InterVarsity Press, 1977. A pamphlet on the relationship between Jesus and Judaism. Its ultimate message is that "... Jewish followers of Yeshua (Jesus) can be that bridge of understanding between the church and the synagogue..." This press is part of the InterVarsity Christian Fellowship, which is itself a missionary group on campus and has published a large number of booklets on the major cults, showing how they deviate from Christianity. They are well-designed and useful material.

LaMagdeleine, Dan. *Jews for Jesus: Organizational Structure and Supporters*, unpublished master's thesis, Berkeley, Calif.: Graduate Theological Union, 1977.

New York State Attorney General, Albany, N.Y.: Lefkowitz, Louis, *Final Report on the Activities of the Children of God*, 1974. One of the few times that a state's attorney general office has investigated a cult. Other states are fearful of freedom of religion violations. Thus, they are reluctant to intervene in these matters.

Porter, Jack Nusan. "Some Political and Legal Aspects of Cults." Paper presented at the Society for the Study of Social Problems, Boston, Mass., August 27, 1979. Discusses the pros and cons of legal and illegal intervention — kidnapping, deprogramming conservatorship, etc. (Available from author.)

Shaw, Steven, and George E. Johnson. "Jews on an Eastern Religious Quest and the Jewish Response," *Analysis* (published by the institute for Jewish Policy Planning and Research), November 1, 1973, No. 41. 14 pages. A well-written and reasoned report on the spiritual search among Jews that often leads them to join religious cults and sects.

Special Section on Cults and Brainwashing. Philadelphia Society of Clinical Psychologists, December 9, 1977. Packet of papers on cult's "brainwashing" from a clinical point of view.

Spiritual Counterfeits Project, Box 4308, Berkeley, CA 94704. A kit of brochures on various cults from Eckankar to the Holy Order of Mans to the Unification Church. Written from a Christian point of view, and well researched and intelligently written. Highly recommended.

Supreme Rabbinic Court of America, Inc. — Commission on Cults and Missionaries. *Unification Church Master File*, 1401 Arcola Ave., Silver Spring, MD 20902. This fascinating document, including a *Cherem*, a writ of ex-communication from the Jewish religion upon *Jewish* leaders of the Unification Church, shows the anti-Semitic nature of the Church through its own writings. This Rabbinical Court excommunicated the following Moonie leaders for engaging in the "physical and spiritual destruction of the Jewish people": Dr. Charles Bergman, Dr. William Bergman, Susan Bergman, Mose Durst (recently appointed director of the American branch), Daniel Feffernan and Joseph Hausner.

Tapes on Christian missionaries, by Rabbi I. Schochet, Kalman Packouz, Maurice Lamm, and others. Star Publications Copy Service, PO box 7768, Long Beach, CA 90807. 1980.

"Toward Our Third Century," Pictorial Issue of *News World*. Tarrytown, N.Y., July 4, 1976. A cleverly and very well done illumination of 120 famous events in America's past, present and future — all used to promote the messiahship of Reverend Sun Myung Moon. The special issue was timed to coincide with the Bicentennial celebrations in the United States.

Unification Church. Response to A. James Rudin's Report, "Jews and Judaism in Reverend Moon's *Divine Principle*," prepared by the Unification Church Department of Public Affairs, Daniel Holdgreiwe, Director, and John Sonneborn. March 1977, 13 pages. An almost line-by-line refutation of Rabbi Rudin's critique. Should be read with Rabbi Rudin's original statement. How much of it is actual refutation and how much an exercise in apologetics or cover-up is ultimately left to the reader.

University Religious Council. "Understanding Cult Involvement" and "Learn to be a Questioner," two pamphlets distributed by the URC, 2311 Bowditch Street, Berkeley, CA 94704. Useful booklets for young people and the helping professions that may prevent youth from joining after they read them.

Notes

1   For extensive materials on this subject, consult the Schomburg Research Center, New York Public Library, 135th Street and Lenox Avenue, New York, NY 10027.

2.   Emphasis on Jewish groups.

ORGANIZATIONAL RESOURCES: WHERE TO TURN FOR HELP

The following provides information of sources of help on cults.

Part I lists anti-cult groups who seek to limit the growth of cults. These groups support such measures as deprogramming and conservatorship in various degrees.

Part II are Jewish anti-cult and missionary groups.

Part III, while not necessarily pro-cult, are groups who support the right of cult members to stay in the cult and who oppose any coercive measures that may impinge on freedom of religion or civil liberties. This "gray area" of the law is quite controversial here, and each group listed has its own interpretation of what constitutes civil liberties.

I.   General Anti-Cult Groups

American Family Foundation
c/o K.H. Barney
PO Box 343
Lexington, MA 02173

Citizens Engaged in Freeing Minds
PO Box 664
Exeter, NH 02833

Citizens Engaged in Reuniting Families
Box 368
Harrison, NY 10528

Citizens' Freedom Foundation
Box 7000-89
1719 Via El Prado
Redondo Beach CA 90277

Committee Engaged in Freeing Minds
Box 5084
Arlington, TX 76011

COPAC
PO Box 3194
Greensboro, NC 27402

Dr. John Clark
Harvard Medical School
25 Shattuck Street
Boston, MA 02115

Ex-Members Against Moon
c/o Steve Hassan
PO Box 62
Brookline, MA 02146

Free Minds, Inc.
PO Box 4216
Minneapolis, MN 55414

Freedom Counseling Center
1633 Old Bay Shore Highway, #265
Burlingame, CA 94010

Institute of Contemporary Christianity
PO Box A
Oakland, NJ 07436

Reconciliation Associates
Dr. Irving Doress
Dr. Jack Nusan Porter
42 Englewood Avenue
Brookline, MA 02146

Return to Personal Choice Inc.
Box 159
Lincoln, MA 01773

Spiritual Counterfeits Project
PO Box 4308
Berkeley, CA 04704

II.   *Jewish Anti-Cult and Missionary Groups*

Agudath Israel of America, Inc.
5 Beekman Street
New York, NY 10038

Anti-Missionary Institute
PO Box 1631
GPO Station 10001
New York, NY 10001

B'nai B'rith Hillel Foundations
1640 Rhode Island Avenue NW
Washington, DC 20036

Chabad–Lubavitch
770 Eastern Parkway
Brooklyn, NY 11213

Cult Hot Line
Jewish Board of Family and Children's Services
1651 Third Avenue
New York, NY 10021

Hineni, Inc.
Rebbetzin Esther Jungreis
Barbara Janov
440 Hungry Harbor Road
North Woodmere, NY 11581

Jews for Jews
c/o Rubin R. Dobin
PO Box 6194
Miami Beach, FL 33154

Lincoln Square Synagogue
200 Amsterdam Avenue
New York, NY 10023

National Conference of Synagogue Youth
Union of Orthodox Jewish Congregations of America
(NCSY/UOJCA)
116 East 27th Street
New York, NY 10016

National Council of Young Israel
3 West 16th Street
New York, NY 10011

Rabbi James Rudin
American Jewish Committee
165 East 56th Street
New York, NY 10022

Task Force on Missionary Activity
Jewish Community Relations Council
Dr. Seymour Lachman
Dr. Martin Dan
111 West 40th Street, #2600
New York, NY 10018

West Coast Jewish Training Project
190 Denslowe Drive
San Francisco, CA 94132

Yavneh
156 Fifth Avenue
New York, NY 10010

III. Pro-Cult Groups

Alliance for the Preservation of Religious Liberty
PO Box 3803
Los Angeles, CA 90028

American Civil Liberties Union (ACLU)
22 East 40ᵗʰ Street
New York, NY 10016 (or local chapters)

APRL
c/o International Society for Krishna Consciousness
3764 Watseka Avenue
Los Angeles, CA 90034

East-West Foundation
17 Station Street
Brookline, MA 02146

Program for the Study of New Religious Movements in America
2451 Ridge Road
Berkeley, CA 94709

Spiritual Community Publications
PO Box 1080, Department G
San Rafael, CA 94902

The Theosophical Society
122 Bay State Road
Boston, MA 02115 (or local chapters)

REFERENCES

American Jewish Committee
165 East 56th Street
New York, NY 10022

American Zionist
4 East 34th Street
New York, NY 10016

Analysis
Institute for Jewish Policy Planning and Research
1776 Massachusetts Avenue NW
Washington, DC 20036

Annals of the American Academy of Political and Social Science
3937 Chestnut Street
Philadelphia, PA 19104

Anti-Defamation League
ADL Bulletin
823 United Nations Plaza
New York, NY 10017

Anti-Missionary Institute
PO Box 1631
GPO Station, NY 10001

Baker Book House
Box 6287
Grand Rapids, MI 49506

Baltimore Jewish Times
2104 North Charles Street
Baltimore, MD 21218

Behrman House
1261 Broadway
New York, NY 10001

Beth Sar Shalom
PO Box 2000
Orangeburg, NY 10962
and Box 1331
Englewood Cliffs, NJ 07632

B'nai B'rith Hillel Foundations
640 Rhode Island Avenue NW
Washington, DC 20036

Broadman Press
127 Ninth Avenue North
Nashville, TN 37234

Brotherhood
National Federation of Temple Brotherhood
838 Fifth Avenue
New York, NY 10021

Christian Herald
40 Overlook Drive
Chappaqua, NY 10514

Commentary
165 East 56th Street
New York, NY 10022

Congress Monthly
15 East 84th Street
New York, NY 10028

Conservative Judaism
3080 Broadway
New York, NY 10027

Dialogue
National Conference of Christians and Jews
43 West 57th Street
New York, NY 10019

Dorset Publishing Company
355 Markham Street
Toronto, Ontario M6G 2K8
CANADA

Encyclopedia Judaica
Keter Publishing House
16 Bet Hadfus Street
P.O.B. 7145
Jerusalem 91071
ISRAEL

Fordham Law Review
School of Law, Fordham University
140 West 62nd Street
New York, NY 10023

Graduate Theological Union
2465 LeConte Avenue
Berkeley, CA 04709

Hadassah Magazine
50 West 58th Street
New York, NY 10019

Hamorah Press
PO Box 48862
Los Angeles, CA 90048

Hineni, Inc.
440 Hungry Harbor Road
North Woodmere, NY 11581

International Society for Krishna Consciousness
3764 Watseka Avenue
Los Angeles, CA 90034

InterVarsity Press
PO Box 1400
Downers Grove, IL 60515

Israel Horizons
150 Fifth Avenue
New York, NY 10011

Jewish Advocate
251 Causeway Street
Boston, MA 02114

Jewish Community Relations Council
111 West 40th Street
New York, NY 10018

Jewish Connection
Syracuse Jewish Federation
321 Seitz Boulevard
201 East Jefferson Street
Syracuse, NY 13202

Jewish Currents
22 East 17th Street
New York, NY 10003

Jewish Digest
1363 Fairfield Avenue
Bridgeport, CT 06605

Jewish Education
114 Fifth Avenue
New York, NY 10011

Jewish Frontier
575 Sixth Avenue
New York, NY 10011

Jewish Observer
5 Beekman Street
New York, NY 10038

Jewish Post and Opinion
101 Fifth Avenue
New York, NY 10003

Jewish Spectator
PO Box 2016
Santa Monica, CA 90406

Jewish Student Press Service
15 East 26ᵗʰ Street
New York, NY 10010

Jewish Week
1 Park Avenue
New York, NY 10016

Jews for Jews
PO Box 6194
Miami Beach, FL 33154

Jonathan David Publishers
68-22 Eliot Avenue
Middle Village, NY 11379

Journal of Jewish Communal Service
15 East 26ᵗʰ Street
New York, NY 10010

Journal of Marital and Family Counseling
924 West Ninth
Upland, CA 91786

Journal for the Scientific Study of Religion
St. John's University
Jamaica, NY 11439

Judaism
15 East 84ᵗʰ Street
New York, NY 10028

Keats Publishing Company
Box 876
36 Grove Street
New Canaan, CT 06840

Keeping Posted
838 Fifth Avenue
New York, NY 10021

Kol Yavneh
25 West 26th Street
New York, NY 10010

KTAV
75 Varick Street
New York, NY 10013

Marriage and Family Review
c/o Haworth Press
149 Fifth Avenue
New York, NY 10010

McGrath Publishing Company
Box 9001
Wilmington, NC 28402

Media and Methods
401 Broad Street
Philadelphia, PA 19108

Midstream
515 Park Avenue
New York, NY 10022

Moment
462 Boylston Street
Suite 301
Boston, MA 02116

National Conference of Synagogue Youth (NCSY)
and Union of Orthodox Jewish Congregations
116 East 27th Street
New York, NY 10016

National Jewish Monthly
1640 Rhode Island Avenue NW
Washington, DC 20036

Pedagogic Reporter
114 Fifth Avenue
New York, NY 10011

Present Tense
165 East 56th Street
New York, NY 10022

Reconciliation Associates
42 Englewood Avenue
Brookline, MA 02146

Reconstructionist
15 West 86th Street
New York, NY 10024

Reform Judaism
838 Fifth Avenue
New York, NY 10021

Religious Education
409 Prospect Street
New Haven, CT 06510

Rudolf Steiner Publications, Inc.
Garber Hill Road
Blauvelt, NY 10913

Sh'ma
PO Box 567
Port Washington, NY 11050

Southern California Law Review
Law Center, University of Southern California
University Park
Los Angeles, CA 90007

Social Compass
Place Montsquieu 1
Boîte 21
1348 Louvain-La-Neuve
BELGIUM

Spiritual Community Publications
PO Box 1080
Department G
San Rafael, CA 94902

Spiritual Counterfeits Project
Box 4308
Berkeley, CA 94704

Union of American Hebrew Congregations (UAHC)
838 Fifth Avenue
New York, NY 10021

United Synagogue Review Quarterly
155 Fifth Avenue
New York, NY 10010

University Press of America
PO Box 19101
Washington, DC 20036 NW

Victor Books
PO Box 1825
Wheaton, IL 60187

Women's American ORT Reporter
1250 Broadway
New York, NY 10001

Worldview
170 East 64th Street
New York, NY 10021

Women's World (B'nai B'rith Women)
1640 Rhode Island Avenue NW
Washington, DC 20036

Zalonka Publications
42 Englewood Avenue
Brookline, MA 02146

Other, more well-known listings of publishers and journals can be found in *Ulrich's International Periodicals Directory* (from R.R. Bowker); *Books in Print*, Title Index, Volume 2, and *Literary Market Place* (also R.R. Bowker). For Jewish items, see the *American Jewish Yearbook*, 165 East 56th Street, New York, NY 10022, and the *Jewish Literary Marketplace*, c/o Arbit Books, 8050 North Port Washington Road, Milwaukee, WI 53217.

ABOUT THE AUTHOR

Jack Nusan Porter is a sociologist, author/editor, and political activist. Born in the Ukraine and raised in Milwaukee, he is a graduate of the University of Wisconsin–Milwaukee, and from Northwestern University, where he received his Ph.D. in Sociology in 1971. He has written over 100 articles, many on Jewish sociology and religion, and has edited several books,[1] among which are *Jewish Radicalism* (with Peter Dreier) and *The Sociology of American Jews*. His writings on cults are cited in the present bibliography.

Dr. Porter has lectured widely on American social problems and political/religious movements, testifying before various government commissions. He has been the recipient of fellowships from the Breadloaf Writers Conference and from the Memorial Foundation for Jewish Culture.

Dr. Porter is a resident of Boston, and the founder of the *Journal of the History of Sociology*, to which he is a current contributor.

Notes

1   His publications are listed in *Contemporary Authors* and other guides.

HANDBOOK OF CULTS, SECTS, & SELF-REALIZATION GROUPS

Compiled by
Jack Nusan Porter, Ph.D.

INTRODUCTION

Historical Background

America has been a country that has always attracted and nurtured religious independence. In many ways we are a deeply religious nation, but we have a history of both bias and tolerance toward new religions. Founded as a haven for persecuted religious minorities such as the Puritans and Quakers, America has also been very uncomfortable with some of its religions. What is remarkable is the tenacity of these groups in the face of severe oppression and their later emergence as not merely accepted but "establishment" religions.

There seems to be a definite sociological cycle at work. First, the group is greeted by various forms of prejudice and persecution, ranging from mild stereotypes to lynching, beatings and enforced discrimination. The victimized group either moves to a more isolated area away from discrimination, or keeps a low profile while living among its victimizers. Prejudice may continue over many decades, but beating and lynching stops, and over time the group's strangeness is ignored or overlooked, and eventually groups, such as the Mormons or the Christian Scientists, which began as persecuted cults or sects, become respectable and established religions, and they in turn now feel superior to the newly emerging cults of today.

From time immemorial, there have been numerous examples in all parts of the world of persecuted sects and cults that pass through these stages and become established churches. A study of history thus leads to some degree of tolerance for the present-day cult phenomenon. We are seeing nothing new, both in world and in American history. However, what is new is the scope of the problem. At no time in history has there emerged so many diverse cults and sects and with so much wealth and appeal. Social scientists had thought that religion was dying out in the United States, that being modern meant a reliance upon reason and science, and that religion meant an atavistic return to superstition and ritualistic mumbo-jumbo. But science and technology have not ushered in a golden age. While doing a great deal of good in so many areas, they have also caused us untold misery — bombs, pollution, nuclear accidents, war. They have not brought us happiness. Faith and philosophy have entered to provide answers that comfort.

Perhaps the growth of religious groups should not have surprised us in the aftermath of Hiroshima, Auschwitz, My Lai, and other "holocausts." Several aspects are surprising: sophistication in the use of marketing, public relations, and media-manipulation that some cults have mastered; the impact of Eastern, non-Christian sects and cults that have proliferated in America; the vastly greater amounts of money collected by cults; the world-wide communications network; and the simple audacity, deception, and outright *chutzpah* of today's cults — all these are new in scope (if not in substance) from earlier periods in American or world history.

Amidst all this seeming chaos and creativity, I hope that this booklet will help explain things so that people can have knowledge — because knowledge is power.

Scope of Handbook

This handbook is a glossary of religious concepts and groups. It is, of course, dated from the moment the reader picks it up. There are hundreds of cults, sects, and religious concepts. In my sources section, I list additional places to where the reader/student can turn. I ask readers to do so if they find something missing or inadequate. This handbook was compiled as a ready reference for people who have heard of a cult, sect or expression, usually Eastern, and who wish a quick definition. Secondly, any glossary or dictionary is idiosyncratic in that certain items appear because the author felt they were interesting or important to him. There is, however, an emphasis on Eastern religions because few Westerners are familiar with such groups.

I have tried to concentrate on major cults and sects and major terms and concepts that may be unknown to most Western readers. I have also kept personalities and psychic or occult terms to a minimum because one could compile a large listing of those alone. I wanted to concentrate on what the public considers cults and sects. I do, however, include a few references to established religions that were once cults or sects. Also, people are indexed according to surname or spiritual name, and honorary titles such as "guru," "swami," "Master," "Doctor," etc., should be disregarded. Thus, Swami Satchidananda would be listed under his surname and not under "swami."

One thing will be striking to readers from the West: the old argument of Monism vs. Dualism. In the West, we separate mind and body, sacred and profane, religion and psychology, spirituality and food, etc. In fact, we separate religion from *most* aspects of life. Traditional religions, especially in the East, make no such distinctions. They do not have a one-a-week religion; religion is a *way of life*, affecting all aspects of life. Thus, this handbook includes groups and individuals who bridge the gap between, for example, psychology and religion and other such dualisms. This may be difficult to accept by Westerners at first, but it is fundamental to the new awakening: all is connected to all — food is politics; eating is religious; playing is love — we are all one. It makes for a very interesting and often startling view of the world.

In any case, please send your corrections, comments, and questions to Jack Nusan Porter, Ph.D.

Sources and Acknowledgments

An excellent companion piece to this handbook is *Kids in Cults: Why They Join, Why They Stay, and Why They Leave* (written by Irvin Doress and Jack Nusan Porter, *RC Associates*, 79 Walnut St. #4, Newton, MA 02460). This booklet contains an excellent bibliography and other sources, especially if you know someone who is in a cult that you think is "bad" for the person. My other booklet, *Jews and the Cults* (Biblio Press, 1981), will also prove useful.

Several groups/books should be consulted: The most comprehensive source on this ever-changing situation is the *Spiritual Community Guide and New Age Directory*, which lists sects, cults, institutes, publications, communes, films, and publishers. *The New Age Directory* is $25, and spiritual guides (for example, *The New Consciousness Source Book #4*, 1979) are $5.95. They are beautifully designed and very useful. Write to: Spiritual Community Publications, P.O. Box 1080, Dept. G, San Rafael, CA 94902.

Another very important collection is *The New Age Dictionary*, edited by Alex Jack, associate editor of *East-West Journal* (write to: Kanthaka Press, P.O. Box 696, Brookline Village, MA 02147 or to the *East-West Journal* directly). I wish to acknowledge the contribution of Alex Jack and the dictionary to this handbook, and I thank him for permission to use certain items. The dictionary costs $5.00, and I highly recommend it. See also Bill Gladstone, "Cults: America's Growth Industry?", *San Francisco Chronicle*, Wednesday, June 6, 1979, and June 8, 1979, "People" section. This was an extremely helpful source for descriptions of several cults mentioned here.

Other source books that were utilized are: Katinka Matson, *The Psychology Today Omnibook of Personal Development*, New York: Wm. Morrow, 1977, $5.95 paperback; Rudolf Steiner, *The Steinerbooks Dictionary of the Psychic, Mystic, Occult*, Blauvelt, N.Y: Rudolf Steiner Publications, 1973; *The Challenge of the Cults*, Philadelphia: Jewish Community Relations Council, 1978; *Spiritual Counterfeits Project* (newsletter and journal), P.O. Box 4308, Berkeley, CA 94704, and *InterVarsity Press* (Downers Grove, IL 60515), which publishes short but useful booklets on the new religions.

It is of course important to go to the religious group itself. It usually has a great deal of literature, and most of it is free. Read it carefully and balance it with other material. *The Encyclopedia Judaica* and the *Encyclopedia Britannica* are good places to begin, as is the growing literature on the new religions, some of which are listed below.

I would also like to publicly thank Dr. Irvin Doress and Professor Harvey Cox, and I recommend M.S. Rosenberg's *Quotations for the New Age*, Secaucus, N.J.; Citadel Press (Lyle Stuart), 1978. Meir Rosenberg has been my eternal goad, and I dedicate this book to him.

Other sources include:

American Heritage Dictionary of the English Language, Boston and New York: Houghton-Mifflin and American Heritage Publishing Company, 1969.

Bullock, Alan and Oliver Stallybrass (eds.), *The Harper Dictionary of Modern Thought*, New York and London: Harper and Row, 1977.

Chutzpah Anthology, San Francisco: New Glide Publications, 1977, $5.95.

Cox, Harvey, *Turning East: The Promise and Peril of the New Orientalism*, New York: Simon and Schuster, 1977.

Eastman, Roger, *The Ways of Religion*, San Francisco: Canfield Press (Harper and Row), 1975.

Enroth, Ronald, *Youth, Brainwashing, and the Extremist Cults*, Grand Rapids Mich.: Zondervan, 1977.

Needleman, Jacob, et al. (eds.), *Religion for a New Generation*, New York: Macmillan, 1973.

Porter, Jack Nusan (ed.), *Jews and the Cults*, Fresh Meadows, N.Y.: Biblio Press, 1981.

Porter, Jack Nusan, and Peter Dreier (eds.), *Jewish Radicalism*, New York: Grove Press/Random House, 1973.

Robbis, Thomas, and Dick Anthony (eds.), *In Gods We Trust*, New Brunswick, N.J.: Transaction Books, 1980.

Rosten, Leo (ed.), *Religions of America*, New York: Simon and Schuster, 1975.

Smith, Huston, *The Religions of Man*, New York: Harper and Row, 1965.

Sparks, Jack, *The Mindbenders: A Look at Current Cults*, Nashville, Tenn.: Thomas Nelson, 1977.

Stein, Jess (ed.), *The Basic Everyday Encyclopedia*, New York: Random House, 1954.

Stoner, Carroll, and JoAnne Parke, *All Gods' Children: The Cult Experience: Salvation or Slavery?*, New York and Middlesex, England: Penguin Books, 1979. (Originally published by Chilton Book Company.)

Theodorson, George A., and Achilles G. Theodorson, *Modern Dictionary of Sociology*, New York: Thomas Y. Crowell (Apollo Eds.), 1969.

<u>GLOSSARY OF TERMS & PEOPLE</u>

Abilitism: a self-realization group founded by Charles Berner, a Californian, in the 1960s. It combines meditation, two-on-two encounters, and psychological self-exposure with a clean, isolated environment. Two-day or five-day group "intensives" are held in the group's *ashram* or community center. Abilitism is an interesting combination of Eastern (Hindu and Buddhist) rituals and Western encounter groups. It has a temporary positive effect in relaxing and cleansing the body. While thriving in the 1960s, this group may have disappeared today, or is found only in California, where its founder lives. Its techniques seem to have influenced Werner Erhard's *est* to some degree. See: ***est.***

acupressure: a Japanese art of healing based on massage and the stimulation of certain points in order to stimulate the flow of "life energy" through the body. See: **Shiatsu.**

acupuncture: a healing art and form of medicine developed in China which is based on the insertion of needles in the body to relieve pain and release blocked "life energy."

The Alamo Christian Foundation: a California cult founded by Tony and Susan Alamo. It was one of the first groups in California to start what has been called the Jesus Movement (in 1968) when they searched for hippies and young people on Sunset Strip in Los Angeles. Today, about 150 members live in sex-segregated communes in Saugus (Los Angeles County) and Alma, Arkansas. Complaints of beatings and slave labor have been voiced about the group. Annual revenues exceed $1.3 million. See: **Jesus People.**

Alexander Technique: a structural integration technique developed by F.M. Alexander; it uses body movement and manipulation to help achieve balance and integrity.

American Family Foundation: an organization founded by family members who have had children in cults plus professionals and laypeople, whose objective is to disseminate information on cults and their impact on young people. Located in Lexington, Massachusetts, the foundation puts out a newspaper and position papers and stresses legal and political influence as well as education to counteract cults. It contains a Center on Destructive Cultism.

AMORC: short for **Ancient and Mystical Order of Rosae Crucis**, a secret society which flourished in the 15th and 16th centuries, allegedly founded by a German named Christian Rosenkreuz ("red cross") about 1430. Their symbol is a rose in the center of a cross. They claim a traditional association with the "Great White Brotherhood" of Egypt, 1500 B.C. Today, known as the Rosicrucian Fellowship, AMORC is a secret religious society, dealing in Christian mysticism and the occult. While disapproving of Spiritualism, members do believe in the existence of a latent sixth-sense which, if cultivated, enables the superphysical realm of the dead to be investigated. AMORC is a worldwide group, with its American center in California. Members are required never to reveal its secrets. See: **Rosicrucian Fellowship.**

Ananda: divine bliss. Chief disciple of the Buddha.

Ananda Marga: literally "path of bliss" — an international socio-spiritual movement founded by Shrii Shrii Anandamurti in 1955. The movement has spread to over 90 countries and many states in the USA. Members practice meditation, personal morality, pure diet, and yoga. In the social sphere, Ananda Marga runs schools, clothing projects, group homes, free kitchens, prison programs, and disaster relief work. Anandamurti was recently charged with conspiring to kill seven former disciples. The charges were dropped, but to protest his imprisonment several European members immolated themselves. Members give 10 percent (or more) of their wages to Ananda, which also sells shampoo, soap, and health food under the Golden Lotus label. Its headquarters recently moved from India to Denver, Colorado. It has about 300 followers in the USA.

Anthroposophy: a religious philosophy founded by social thinker Rudolf Steiner. It postulates the existence of a spiritual world comprehensible to "pure thinking" but fully accessible only to the higher faculties of knowledge latent in every person. The Anthroposophical Society, founded in 1912 by Steiner, engages in farming, gardening, schools for maladjusted children, scientific research, and therapy. See: **Rudolf Steiner; theosophy.**

Apostles of Infinite Love: founded in France in 1952 as a breakaway Roman Catholic sect that denounced the Pope for his imagined connections to freemasonry. Founder Michel Collin, a defrocked priest, called himself Pope Clement XV. Followers of the Apostles number about 1,000 and are found as far afield as Vermont, New Brunswick, Alberta (Canada), and Europe.

100

Aquarian Minyan: a West Coast, California-based Jewish countercultural and spiritual group that acts as an alternative to non-Jewish cults and sects. Located in Berkeley, California. See: **Jewish counter culture; B'nai Or.**

Arica: Founded in 1971 by Oscar Ichazo, Arica uses methods called "trainings," designed by Ichazo, to attain a state of self-realization in the shortest possible time. These methods include meditation and physical exercise. Arica is a place in Chile, where Ichazo is from.

Ashram: a religious center, combining a place of worship (a temple); a community center (offices and eating facilities); and a center for meditation and study all in one. A Buddhist term.

Assagiolo, Roberto (1888-1974): Italian psychologist and founder of psychosynthesis. See: **psychosynthesis.**

Astara: More than 100 lessons in world religion, philosophy, nutrition, mysticism, and yoga comprise Astara's "book of Life," which traces a course from prebirth to afterlife. Drs. Robert and Earlyne Chaney, who formed Astara in 1951, maintain a ten-acre retreat in Upland (San Bernardino County, California). At least 25,000 members have paid $10 membership fees in 90 countries.

astral projection: out-of-body experiences, usually occurring during sleep, wherein one's "double" leaves the body and travels elsewhere.

astrology: an ancient form of divination. Initiated by the Babylonians and later expanded by 2nd century B.C. Greeks, with later refinement by ancient Egyptians, Hebrews, Arabs, and medieval Europeans. Astrology is an occult science based on the influence of the stars and planets. By using an individual's horoscope, an astrologer

101

can obtain a constellation of the zodiac utilizing the 12 "houses" (Leo, Aquarius, etc.) which show the relative positions of the planets and signs at a particular time, making it possible to describe and predict one's personality and favorable times for action or inaction.

atman: a Sanskrit term that means "imperishable," that which holds everything, the innermost self, a Western approximation to the concept of the "soul." Atman is also the divine spark within a person or object, similar to Brahman ("world soul" or the "absolute").

Aurobindo, Sri (1872-1950): Indian philosopher and guru, author of *The Life Divine*.

avatar: Hindu term for the "descent" to earth or the reincarnation of a supreme deity into human or animal form. For example: Krishna, Rama, Zoroaster, or Jesus. In some religions, some deities can be reincarnated into many forms, from a fish to a hero.

Baal Shem Tov (1700-1760): the founder of the orthodox, pietistic Jewish sect the Hasidim. The Baal Shem Tov (Hebrew for "maser of the Good Name) was a simple worker who in the 1750s decided that a direct, exuberant, and pure approach to God was necessary. The many Hasidic *rebbes* today take their lineage directly from him. The original name of this Ukrainian-born founder was Israel ben Eliezer. See: **Hasidim, rebbe, Lubavitcher Rebbe, Satmar Rebbe.**

baba: Sanskrit for "father."

Back to Godhead: the magazine of the Hare Krishna movement. Founded in 1964 by its founder, A.C. Bhaktivedanta Swami Prabhupada. See: **ISKCON; Hare Krishna.**

Bahai: Bahai members follow the teachings of Baha'u'lah who in Persia in 1863 proclaimed himself an avatar. He taught that the universe was one, that all people on earth were one, that spiritual love should unite all people. Bahai is found throughout the USA and Canada, with national headquarters in Wilmette, Illinois, a suburb of Chicago. An extremely beautiful center is also found in Haifa, Israel.

Bardo Thodol: the *Tibetan Book of the Dead*, a Tibetan holy book.

Berg, David Brandt: the founder, in the late 1960s, of the Children of God. Berg, who also calls himself Moses David, was a one-time Bible teacher and itinerant evangelist. His parents were active in the Christian and Missionary Alliance before and after World War II. After the war, Berg fell out with the leaders of the church he was pastoring, and, with much bitterness and contempt for organized religion, he felt that God had a mission for him. He eventually founded COG, the Children of God, with himself as its master and spiritual guide. See: **Children of God.**

Bhagavad Gita (Song of God): part of the Indian epic Mahabharata: a Hindu sacred writing sung by Lord Krishna, showing devotion to a personal god. It is also a compendium of Upanishadic teachings. Strict Brahmins do not accept it, but it is the centerpiece of the Hare Krishna sect/cult in the USA and elsewhere. See: **Hare Krishna.**

Bhagwan Shree Rajneesh (1931-1990): From Poona, India, comes Rajneesh, author of *Nothing to Lose But Your Head*, and sex guru who teaches that people should say yes to every bodily impulse. His 35,000 or so disciples around the world wear orange (the color of sexual energy), a string of 109 beads (representing the 108 names of God plus one more for Rajneesh), and practice one of the guru's meditations daily. See: **Rajneesh Shree Bhagwan.**

Bhajan, Yogi (1929-2004), a.k.a. Harbhajan Singh Yogi: Indian-born Sikh teacher; founder of the 3HO Foundation, which stands for Health, Happy, Holy Organization. Yogi Bhajan (Siri Singh Sahib) came to America in 1969, recognizing the need to balance the technology of Western industry with the technology of Eastern spirituality. See: **Happy, Holy, Healthy Organization.**

Bhaktivedanta, A.C. (1895-1977): known as Swami Prabhupada, a Bengali-born writer, teacher, and founder of the Hare Krishna movement. Author of *The Bhagavad Gita As It Is* and other works. See: **Hare Krishna; Bhagavad Gita.**

bhakti yoga: a branch, one of seven paths, of yoga. It is the path of devotion, of a personal relationship with God; utilized by members of the Hare Krishna organization.

Bible Speaks: Carl Stevens started Bible Speaks in the late 1960s. Their World Outreach missionaries have entered Russia on the pretext of being college students and may soon enter China as well. Their main source of funds is a daily radio show called Telephone Time, which is heard by millions across the country. Headquartered in Lenox, Massachusetts, there are about 1,000 members and 700 students.

bioenergetics: a therapeutic method developed by Alexander Lowen which emphasizes expressive mobility and the easy flow of energy in breathing, sound, and posture. Psychological blocks are caused by blockage in the "body armor." Heavily influenced by the works of the Austrian psychiatrist Wilhelm Reich. See: **Reich, Wilhelm.**

biofeedback: a technique and a science of listening to amplified brain waves and learning to consciously control them in order to achieve peace of mind, reduction in stress, lowered pulse rates and blood pressure. The technique utilizes a lightweight gadget that fits onto the head with electrodes properly secured and connected to headphones.

Black Baptists: a wide array of Pentecostal religions, combining Christianity, African elements, and the slave experience; a major religion among American blacks.

Black Jews: Several sects among African-Americans utilize Jewish forms of worship and tradition but are co-mingled with the black experience. There are congregations of black Jews in Harlem, Chicago, and other major American cities. Several feel their roots go back to Ethiopia, where the *Falashas*, a Jewish sect live; still others are Rastafarians, who view the late Emperor Haile Selassie I as their messiah. (Selassie's original name was Ras Tafari Makkonen.) Still others are descendants of Jewish slave-owners in the American south or Caribbean. Several thousand live in the United States. See: **Rastafarians.**

Black Muslims: a black religious sect that has murky origins in northern American urban centers. Its early leader, Elijah Muhammad, preached a gospel of black self-realization and pride, a return to one's African (and Moslem) roots, hatred of whites, and "black power." It was despised and oppressed by American police and FBI agents. Today, it has, under Elijah Muhammad's son, changed and become more tolerant of whites. Its most famous members were Malcolm X (who renounced it after his pilgrimage to Mecca) and Muhammad Ali.

Blavatsky, Mme. Helena Petrovna (1831-1891): Russian-born co-founder, with Colonel H.S. Olcott, of the Theosophical Society, with its first headquarters in Adyar, India. Not only did she live a mysterious and extraordinarily adventurous life, but her talents as a leader, medium, and writer won her many important disciples — Annie Besant, Rudolf Steiner, and Krishnamurti. Author of *The Secret Doctrine, Isis Unveiled,* and other works. See: **Theosophy, Theosophical Society.**

"blissed-out": term, coined by the Divine Light Mission, to mean totally joyous and complete. The opposite of "freaked-out."

B'nai Or: an organization devoted to God, Consciousness, Torah, and the harmonious development of the whole Jewish person. Founded by Rabbi Zalman Schacter, it stresses community, study, spiritual expression, and religious creativity as an alternative to cults. See: **Rabbi Zalman Schacter.**

B'nai Yeshua: a sect of "Jews for Jesus" that believes one can be a complete and happy Jew and still accept Jesus as the messiah. There are a few such sects in the USA and elsewhere. Often, they are seen as missionaries to the Jews; more often Jews despise them.

bodhisattva: Sanskrit for "enlightening being," one who seeks enlightenment for all living things by postponing one's own final nirvana to assist others. See: **nirvana.**

Brahman: a difficult word to define: "world soul," the "absolute"; also, a member of the noblest Hindu caste. See: **atman.**

brainwashing: a difficult word to define properly, but essentially it means any attempt to coerce individuals into joining a cult through deception, "love-bombing," sleep deprivation, and indoctrination. It is the counterpart of deprogramming. See: **deprogramming, "love-bombing."**

Brand, Stewart (1938-   ): the California creator of *The Whole Earth Catalog;* ecology activist and writer-editor.

Brown, Norman O. (1913-2002): a countercultural writer and thinker who eventually taught at the University of California–Santa Cruz; author of *Love's Body, Life Against Death* and *Closing Time.*

Bubba Free John (1939-2008), a.k.a. Adi Da Samraj: a religious leader and retired head of the Dawn Horse Communion. His original name was Franklin Albert Jones.

Buber, Martin (1878-1965): German-Jewish religious philosopher, mystic, Zionist, and peace advocate. Translated the Bible into German. Taught at the Hebrew University in Jerusalem in later years. Author of *I and Thou, Tales of the Hasidim,* and many other works. See: **Hasidism.**

Buddha: Sanskrit for "awakened one." Siddhartha Gautama, chief spiritual leader of Buddhism, who lived in the 5th and 6th century B.C.

Cao-Dai: Vietnamese way of life combining Taoism, Buddhism, and Christianity. This sect's prophets include Mark Twain and Victor Hugo.

Campus Crusade for Christ: a spiritual movement that attempts to bring Jesus into the lives of college students and teachers. It is also quite active with athletic players.

Carlebach, Rabbi Shlomo (1925-1994): a Jewish singer, composer, and traveling troubadour who brought the joys of the spirit to audiences in the United States, Canada, and Israel. Through song, he brought young Jews back to Judaism.

Castaneda, Carlos (1935-1998): California anthropologist and spiritual apprentice whose books were very popular with young people of all ages in the counterculture. They include *The Teachings of Don Juan, Takes of Power,* and *A Separate Reality.*

"centering": a spiritual and psychological technique (actually many techniques) to find a physical, emotional, mental, and psychic region of inner peace and harmony.

Chabad Hasidim (or Chasidim): a movement of ultra-Orthodox Jews who are members of the Hasidic sect centered in New York City around the spiritual leadership of the Lubavitcher Rebbe, Menachem Mendel Schneerson. The goal of this group is to educate Jews into a deeper appreciation of their heritage and ritual. So-called Chabad Houses can be found in major cities in the world, usually near a college campus. They are, in essence, missionaries of Jews to Jews.

chakra: Sanskrit for "wheel," the center of spiritual energy.

chanting: a musical mode of expression that is relaxing to the participant. Can consist of songs, repetitious sounds or words, or sing-song.

charisma; charismatic: a person blessed (or cursed) with special endowments, gifts or character that attract people; a certain "gift of the gods." This power can be used for either good or evil; for example, a Jesus, a John F. Kennedy, or a Hitler.

Children of God (COG) (now Family International): a Jesus movement founded by David Berg in the late 1960s. Berg, also called Moses Berg, age 65, began proselytizing among hippies in California. He led a flock of 160 out of that state in 1969 after receiving a revelation that it would sink into the sea. In 1973,

Beg had another vision that the comet Kohoutek would destroy North America, and, at his urging, most of his followers left for Europe. COG believed the world would end in 1993. At one time they had an estimated 5,000 members in 800 colonies, most of them outside the USA. It was also called the Church of God. See: **David Brandt Berg, "Mo" Letters.**

Chinmoy, Sri (1931-2007): Bengali spiritual leader, artist, poet, founder of UN Meditation Center.

Christian Scientist: In 1879, fifteen people, students of Mary Baker Eddy, the founder of the church, met in the Boston area to form the First Church of Christ, Scientist. The church believes in the treatment of disease through mental and spiritual means, especially the teachings of Jesus. This church is a good example of a cult that later became an established church. Its headquarters are still in Boston, and they publish the *Christian Science Monitor.* Mrs. Eddy's doctrinal text is *Science and Health with Key to the Scriptures*, designed for use in concordance with the Holy Bible, King James Version. See: **Eddy, Mary Baker.**

Church of Armageddon: another name for the Love Family cult.

Church of Bible Understanding: Stuart Traill sold and reconditioned old vacuum cleaners until he "found Jesus" in 1968. Three years later he was head of a band of Christian fundamentalists in Pennsylvania whom he baptized the Forever Family. This name was changed in 1976 because Traill's divorce made the name inappropriate. In Montreal, New York and New England, the members own a carpet-cleaning company, Christian Brothers Cleaning Service. They have about 2,000 followers.

Church of Hakeem: The Rev. Hakeem Abdul
Rasheed's "Dare to be Rich" success program enticed
about 9,000 Californians to chant "richer faster,
richer faster" and invest $500 to become "ministers
of increase." After some early donors received back
400 percent of their money, he coaxed more than $20
million from his audiences. Law officials said the church
was a pyramid scheme, and a federal grand jury in San
Francisco indicted Rasheed in the late 1970s for fraud.
Rasheed said, "The goal of this church is to make 10,000
millionaires." It seems that the Oakland-based Rasheed
was the only one to prosper.

Church of the Living Word: Also known as the
"Walk," this is a revelationary Christian cult led by John
Robert Stevens. See: **Stevens, John Robert.**

Church of the Redeemer: a Houston Episcopal
community where 180 of 800 "born again" Christian
members lived together in 29 houses and pooled all or
part of their wages. Other such communities existed in
Ann Arbor, Michigan; Washington, D.C.; and Augusta,
Georgia.

"claiming the ground": the term used by Witness
Lee and his church for building a church in a particular
are and proselytizing members. See: **Local Church of
Witness Lee.**

Confucius (551-479 B.C.): a Chinese philosopher,
founder of Confucianism, a system of moral philosophy
which includes the concept of the "Golden Rule," stress
on the "middle way," avoidance of extremes, devotion
to parents, and a comprehensive form of government.
Originally a secular political and social philosophy, it later
added religious beliefs. Confucianism was very influential,
not only on Taoism and Buddhism, but also Judaism and
Christianity.

coven: an enclave consisting of thirteen witches, including a high priestess and six mixed couples. See: **wicca; witchcraft.**

Cox, Harvey (1929-   ): a writer and Professor Emeritus of Harvard Divinity School. His books include *The Secular City, The Seduction of the Spirit, Turning East: The Promise and Peril of the New Orientalism.*

cult: a religious group that is often a breakaway sect of an established religion. It differs from a sect in that it has devoted attachment to one leader, sometimes strange and esoteric rituals, and a millennial vision of the world. However, certain sects have such elements as well. Today, the term is one of disapprobation and reproach. One could, tongue-in-cheek, say that a cult is a sect that has not yet been accepted as a church.

darshan: Hindu term for the physical sight of the guru. Used by Divine Light Mission.

Davis, Rabbi Maurice (1921-1993): a New York rabbi who specialized in reclaiming young people from contemporary religious cults. He was active in an anti-cult group called CERF, Citizens Engaged in Reuniting Families.

Davis, Rennie (1941-   ): a prominent anti-war leader, one of the "Chicago 8" who went on trial in 1969 for his politics and lifestyle, but who later became a leader in the Divine Light Mission. See: **Divine Light Mission.**

Dederich, Charles E. "Chuck", Sr. (1913-1997): founder of California drug rehabilitation center, Synanon, in 1960s. In the late 1970s, however, this retreat center for drug and alcohol addicts turned into a violent, anti-social cult.

deprogramming: a vague term that describes the process by which a person is brought out a cult — by means of talking, influencing, or kidnapping and counter-brainwashing. Controversial, sometimes illegal. See: **brainwashing.**

dervish: a sufi dancer; in popular terms a dancer who moves in a circle so fast he or she bores a hole in the sand or ground. See: **Sufi; Sufism.**

devotees: followers of the Hare Krishna Movement.

dharma: Sanskrit for the law, the truth, and the way in Hinduism; the teachings of Buddha.

dharmadhatu: seed or potentiality of truth; a local chapter and ashram of Trungpa Rinpoche's Vajradhatu movement. See: **Rinpoche Chogyam Trungpa.**

dharmakaya: Sanskrit for "law body," highest of the three bodies of Buddha, representing absolute truth.

dhati: Hindu term for the flowing garment used by males. Also worn by members of the Hare Krishna group.

Dianetics: literal meaning "through thought." This is the Science of Mental health founded by L. Ron Hubbard. It is the science on which Scientology is built — a pseudo-psychological, pseudo-scientific science of mental well-being. See: **Scientology; Hubbard, L. Ron.**

Divine Light Mission: a spiritual organization founded by Param Sant Satgurudev Shri Hans Ji Maharaj in Badrinath, India. The leader, until his mother deposed him, was Guru Maharaj Ji (1960-). This cult was quite wealthy with its, at one time, 50,000 members. Guru Maharaji was attracted to fast cars, diamonds, and blondes. He owned an estate in Malibu and a "flashy pad" in Denver. Initiates, called "premies," could attain oneness with the universe through four meditative techniques: (1) close your eyes to see the light; (2)

close your ears to hear the music; (3) roll your tongue back into your mouth to taste the "divine nectar"; and (4) concentrate on "primordial vibrations" to receive God's word. There were about 200 ashrams in North America with national headquarters in Denver, Colorado. However, since the fall of the "Perfect Master," young Guru Maharaj Ji, the organization itself fell upon hard times.

Divine Principle: the theological philosophy of the Unification Church of Rev. Sun Myung Moon. See: **Unification Church; Moo, Sun Myung.**

DMA: For people who "are ready to reach for the higher possibilities in their lives," this was a self-realization growth group based in Boston, New York City, San Francisco, and other cities.

Doomsday Cult: the name of an actual cult founded in 1978 by Roch (Moses) Theriault, age 31. He and a group of 16 others were certain the world was ending. They holed up in a log cabin in Quebec to await the apocalypse. They may still be there.

doomsday cults: religious groups that feel that the end of the world is near and that one should prepare for its eventual doom. Only a select few will survive. The Children of God (Family International) is a good example of a doomsday cult.

Druids: members of an order of Celtic priests, poets, healers and judges in pre-Christian England, Ireland, and France. What today are called "witches" harken back to Druidic times.

"East Turners": a term used by Harvey Cox, Harvard University theologian, to describe the process and movement of Western people looking toward the East (Japan, Korea, China, India) for spiritual techniques and religious answers. See: **Cox, Harvey.**

East-West Foundation: A macrobiotic educational group founded by Michio Kushi in 1973. Centered in Brookline, Mass., the group publishes a journal, sponsors classes and symposia on diet and health, and owns food stores. See: **macrobiotics.**

East-West Journal: a journal devoted to ecological spiritual, and socio-psychological issues of the day, published by the East-West Foundation in Brookline, Mass.

Eckankar: Literally "co-worker with God," it is a group that practices an ancient science called "soul travel." It was established in Las Vegas in 1965 by the late Paul Twitchell, a former journalist. Students (called "chelas") originally paid $65 a year for seven years of introduction, then $40 in annual membership fees. Members say they leave their bodies at home when the escape the physical realm to explore the "upper planes." Allegedly, three million people practice Eckankar. The group, now led by a man named Harold Klemp, has its international headquarters in Chanhassen, Minnesota, southwest of Minneapolis.

Eddy, Mary Baker: the founder and first/only spiritual leader of the Christian Science Church. See: **Christian Scientist.**

ego; egolessness: Ego is the self, the "I," the self-consciousness of the individual. Some would say it means "soul." Others would define it as the futile effort to secure happiness or the succession of confusions producing an illusory sense of self. Its opposite is egolessness, the absence of all preconceptions, reference points, landmarks, and sense of identity of what is and what should be; the recognition that ego is impermanent.

E-meter: in Scientology, and electronic instrument that measures the mental state or change of state in an individual.

encounter groups: a new development in psychology in the 1960s wherein strangers (or friends) share interpersonal feelings and directly experience those feelings and thoughts in the group. Sometimes combined with other techniques such as gestalt, bioenergetics, dance, psychosynthesis, and the Feldenkrais method.

Ephrata community: a utopian community founded by Johann Beissel in Lancaster County, Pennsylvania (1728-1900), which is today called "Amish" country. Based on the principles of vegetarianism, pacifism, and monasticism.

Erhard, Werner (1935-): Original name was Jack Rosenberg, former salesman. Founder of *est.* See: *est.*

Erickson, Milton H. (1901-1980): Called the most influential hypnotherapist of our time, his techniques included methods of indirect suggestions and deep trance applicable for such symptoms as pain, anxiety, writing and speaking blocks, and habit disorders such as smoking and overeating.

Esalen Institute: one of the earliest and most influential "growth centers" in the United States. Located in a beautiful setting in Big Sur, California, it sponsors a wide range of humanistic experiences: workshops, classes, etc.

***est* (Erhard Seminars Training):** The *est* training was a 60-hour "educational experience" which created an opportunity for people to realize their potential to transform the quality of their lives. Created by the American Werner Erhard in 1971, it was a powerful series of group encounters that attempted to strip away the layers of façade and self-deceit and lead the individual to take responsibility for his/her life. Graduates of the *est* seminars maintained that, while it did not cure all problems, it did work. The training, usually held in hotel rooms, was quite expensive — a $300.00 tuition rate at one time. The legal corporate name was the *est, an educational corporation,* and *est* offices were found in all major United States cities. It was quite a successful self-realization group—with more than 120,000 "graduates" as of 1977—until its dissolution in 1981. The last training was held in 1984. See: **Erhard, Werner.**

Evangelical Christians: Christians that believe in the literal interpretations of the Bible, the Gospels, or the New Testament. They emphasize salvation by faith. Revival meetings are commonly held.

The Farm: Acid guru Stephen Gaskin conducted a weekly hippie gathering in San Francisco called Monday Night Class. When he left in 1970 for a speaking tour of the United States, a caravan of 65 vans and school buses followed him, finally settling on 1,750 acres near Summertown, Tennessee. At its peak, 1,200 to 1,600 followers lived there, and another 900 lived on 15 other farms in the United States and Guatemala; today it has approximately 175 residents. Gaskin's wife, Ina May, and her crew of 12 midwives delivered more than 1,000 babies of visitors at no charge. All members are vegetarian and involved with relief work. Most practice a mix of puritanical Christianity, Zen, and naturalist ethics (no drugs, tobacco, birth control, divorce or cutting the hair). See: **Gaskin, Stephen.**

Father Devine (1875-1965): The Rev. M.J. Divine (George Baker) had 1.5 million followers in the 1930s and a multi-million-dollar empire that included a 73-acre Philadelphia estate. Since his death in 1965, his second wife, Mother Devine, tried to hold this black cult intact.

Followers were asked to pay all bills immediately and never buy anything on credit. They were also celibate. Also called the Kingdom of Peace, the cult is now known as the International Peace Mission Movement.

Feldenkrais method: a method in body movement and self-awareness developed by an Israeli, Moshe Feldenkrais. He states that physical troubles are related to the misuse of the body. Akin to T'ai Chi and the bioenergy theories of Wilhelm Reich.

Fisher-Hoffman Process: Also called the Hoffman Quadrinity Process, this is an intensive 13-week highly directive form of learning, experienced on four levels of meaning: intellectual, emotional, spiritual, and physical. This is made possible by removing the layers of adopted programming learned in childhood and by releasing the emotional attachment to negative patterns. This allows people to experience their essential identity — which is a center of pure love. Headquarters of the Hoffman Institute Foundation, which runs this program, are in San Francisco with workshops held on campuses and centers in other parts of the country.

"fronts": Certain religious cults will maintain political, cultural, and even athletic groups under other names. The Unification Church is especially adept at having many such "fronts." They are directly controlled by the church but they often fool outsiders.

Foundation, The: the new name for "The Process." See: **Process, The.**

Foundation Faith of God: The Foundation Faith was founded in 1974 when a number of ministers broke away from the Process Church, a Christian street ministry preoccupied with Satanism. The 300 American followers raised money with radio shows, including "The Kingdom Crusade," "The Glory Road Crusade," and "The Jewish

Crusade for Jesus." International headquarters were in Phoenix, Arizona. See: **Process, The.**

Fundamentalism: orthodox religious beliefs, usually referred to Christians, based on a literal interpretation of the Bible. See: **Evangelical Christians.**

Gaskin, Stephen (1936-): American guru and "farm beatnik"; founder of the American Kibbutz, the Farm, which is located in Summertown, Tennessee. He started preaching in San Francisco, gathered together a caravan of buses and people, stopping along the way, and eventually found a place in Tennessee for his farm. See: **Farm, The.**

Geller, Uri (1946-): Israeli psychic and "mind bender." He also bends spoons by rubbing them or at a distance, stops or starts clocks and watches. He has also alleged experienced moving through space from one city to another. Author of *My Story.* It's quite possible.

"getting it": an *est* term for realizing your potential or reaching your goal of (temporary) self-realization. See: *est.*

Ginsberg, Allen (1926-1997): Jewish-American poet of the 1950s Beat Generation who later became a guru to Eastern spiritual countercultural groups in the USA and Canada in the 1960s and 1970s. Ginsberg has also become something of a gay activist as well. His most famous book of poetry is *Howl.*

ginseng: a kind of oriental root out of which a tea is made that has powers to "heal and soothe the nervous system" and to bring one closer to love. It is alleged that the Unification Church of Reverend Moon is a major grower and distributor of the root.

glossolalia: speaking in tongues, as if in some kind of trance; the words of the "spirit" speaking through the mouth of the person. Found among "Jesus People" and other fundamentalist Christian groups. See: **Xenoglossy.**

God: a controlling, superhuman power entitled to obedience, reverence, and worship; the perfect, omnipotent ruler of the universe; creator of all life; principal object of faith and love in monotheistic religions; to some, the vital force that moves the world; the "Great Spirit"; the "Supreme Being"; the "Pure Energy."

Godhead: divinity; the quality or state of being a god or of being divine.

Great Heart Buddhist Monastery: Tyndale Martin, the son of an evangelist who got rich in Montreal land deals, proclaimed himself the Panchen Lama of Tibet and founded a monastery in 1970. A powerfully built, magnetic man in his thirties, he once lived in the female wing with eleven disciples with whom he practiced Tantric yoga sexual exercises. Six of the young women bore children by him. The male group, which obtained grants from the Roman Catholic Church, went into decline after the existence of the female followers became known. Tyndale told his harem that if anything happened to him it would be better for their spiritual health if they killed themselves.

Green, Rabbi Arthur (1941-   ): a charismatic leader in the Jewish counterculture; one of the founders of the Havurot Shalom in Boston. Today he is a professor in the non-denominational rabbinical program at Hebrew College in Boston. See; **Havurot Shalom; Jewish counterculture.**

Gurdjieff, George Ivanovitch (1872-1949): Russian-born occultist and religious teacher. He wrote a cosmological epic based on a legend of Beelzebub banished to the solar system. (Beelzebub is another name

119

of the devil, one of the chief fallen angels and second only to Satan in power.) He inspired Peter D. Ouspensky, who developed and disseminated Gurdjieff's teachings and methods throughout the Western world. There has even been a movie based on Gurdjieff's life. See: **Ouspensky, Peter D.**

guru; gurudev: spiritual master or teacher. Hindu term.

Hanuman Foundation: The guru of this group is Baba Ram Dass (formerly Richard Alpert). He lost many of his followers following a break with his "Divine Mother," Joyce Green of Brooklyn, N.Y., but his books continued to sell. Joyce Green, however, claimed to have 200 followers in "Joya Houses" in New York, Florida, and California.

Hannah Lowe's New Testament Missionary Fellowship: a small New York City-based cult, drawing top students from the Columbia University area. The cult is mentioned in Ted Patrick's book *Let Our Children Go!*

Happy, Holy, Healthy Organization: The 3 HO organization, a secular branch of the Sikh religion, 12 million followers worldwide, offers courses in prenatal yoga, vegetarian cooking, and massage. Founded by Yogi Bhajan.

Hare Krishna: a chant in praise of the God, Krishna. The actual words are: "Hare Krishna, Hare Krishna, Krishna Krishna, Hare Hare, Hare Rama, Hare Rama, Rama Rama, Hare Hare…"

Hare Krishna Movement (International Society for Krishna Consciousness): Founded by His Divine Grace Bhaktivedanta Swami Prabhupada in 1966 in New York City, the group has grown rapidly since then, and allegedly had 50,000 US members and millions in India plus total assets of over $50 million at one point. One of the most well-known sects in the world with their shaved heads, saffron robes, and chanting, it is actually a Hindu cult.

Hasidism (or Chasidism): a sect of orthodox Jewish mystics founded by the Baal Shem Tov in Poland (bout 1750) in opposition to the formalistic Judaism and ritual laxity. Hebrew for "pious ones," Hasidim are divided into many sub-sects, each with its own spiritual leader, called the *rebbe*. They are fond today in various American, Israeli, and British cities, and are growing in number. See **rebbe; Lubavitch Hasidim; Satmar Hasidim.**

Hatha Yoga: yoga carried out through work on the body; in a crude sense — through exercise.

Havurot Movement: a religious movement among young Jews, originating in the United States in the late 1960s. The movement believes in communal services with innovations such as participation from all members regardless of sex, age, or status, and an openness to creative forms of prayer.

Havurat Shalom: Hebrew for "Fellowship of Peace," this Somerville, Massachusetts, based group was one of the first *havurot* in the United States and Canada, and a prototype of others that followed. It was founded in the late 1960s by several rabbis and laypeople and still exists today.

Hebrew Science: the Jewish version of Christian Science, using prayer and conviction to heal.

Heschel, Abraham Joshua (1907-1972): one of the leading modern Jewish theologians. Descended from Orthodox Hassidic roots, Heschel was also a Jewish activist who felt that religion and social action go hand-in-hand. Along with Martin Buber, he could be considered the major Jewish philosopher of religion to have had an impact on Christian theology in this century. His books include *Man is Not Alone* and *God in Search of Man.*

Hesse, Hermann (1877-1962): German mystical author whose books were highly influential on the countercultural (hippie) movement of the late 1960s. His works include *Siddhartha,* a novel on the life of Buddha; *Beneath the Wheel; Demian;* and *Steppenwolf.* He won the Nobel Prize in Literature in 1946.

hippies: a cultural movement of the 1960s that started on the West Coast of the United States and traveled round the world. Its adherents practice peace, love, and self-reliance. Also called "Long-haired freaks." See: **Yippies, New Left.**

Hofmann, Dr. Albert (1906-2008): Swiss chemist who developed LSD in 1943. See: **LSD.**

Hoffman, Abbie: a 1960s countercultural leader and one of the founders of the yippies. He was one of the "Chicago 8" who went on trial. See: **Yippies; New Left.**

holistic: something whole, total; treating the entire person or object, as in holistic medicine and using yoga acupuncture, massage, meditation, dance/music therapy, herbs, with minimal use of drugs or surgery, treating the mind as well as the body.

Holy Order of MANS: a fairly new and fast-growing spiritual group, founded in San Francisco in 1968 by Earl Blighton, a 65-year-old ex-engineer. It mimics a Roman Catholic priestly order but is co-ed and quite occultist. Brothers and sisters take vows of poverty, humility, and purity. They publish a journal called *Golden Nuggets.* MANS is an acronym of four Greek letters. There are about 750 members in the cult.

Holy Spirit Association for the Unification of World Christianity: the full name of the Unification Church of Rev. Sun Myung Moon. See: **Unification Church.**

House of Love and Prayer: a religious center founded by Rabbi Shlomo Carlebach in the 1960s that combined study, spiritual prayer, and outreach to young Jews. It was located in San Francisco. See: **Carlebach, Rabbi Shlomo.**

Hubbard, L. Ron (1911-1986): the founder and major spiritual and ideological leader of Scientology. See: **Scientology; Dianetics.**

I Am Ashram: a spiritual movement in Canada founded by Sri Mata Atmanada in 1970.

Ichazo, Oscar (1931-   ): Bolivian-born spiritual teacher, founder of Arica. See: **Arica.**

I Ching: Chinese for "Book of Changes," a Chinese oracle consisting of 64 hexagrams, cast by manipulating 50 yarrow stalks or coins. Its authorship is attributed to Fu Hsi, circa 2900 B.C., and collected by the Duke of Chou, circa 1500 B.C., with commentaries by Confucius.

indoctrination: a term used by foes of religious cults to describe the means by which instruction is given into the theories and beliefs of the religion. Actually, this is a mild term — "brainwashing" is more commonly used. See: **brainwashing.**

Inner Light Foundation: a non-profit and non-denominational organization founded by Betty Bethards, a California psychic, spiritual healer, and meditation teacher. The main purpose of the group is to help awaken "intuitional and spiritual awareness" through meditation.

Institute of Harmonious Development of Man: Gurdjieff's school in Fontainebleau, France, until 1924. See: **Gurdjieff.**

Institute of Mentalphysics: spiritual center, founded by Edwin J. Dingle with headquarters in Yucca Valley, California.

Institute of Noetic Sciences: consciousness research center in Palo Alto, California.

Integral Yoga: a system of yoga developed by Sri Aurobindo that stresses bringing supramental powers of divine consciousness down into the ignorance of mind, life, and body in order to transform and create a divine life in matter.

Integral Yoga Institute: a yoga movement founded by the Swami Satchidananda in 1966 with its main center in Pomfret Center, Connecticut.

ISKON: acronym for the International Society for Krishna Consciousness, the formal name for the Hare Krishna Movement. See: **Hare Krishna Movement.**

Jehovah: a Hebrew term for God. The proper pronunciation of the word is so powerful it can never be used by ordinary Jews or Christians. See: **Yahweh.**

Jehovah's Witnesses: a Christian missionizing sect, founded in the United States but spread throughout the world. It is fundamentalist in tradition and has a powerful "doomsday" element, an end-to-this-world perspective, within its theology.

"Jesus Freaks": a term, sometimes pejorative, for Jesus People, members of the Jesus Movement. See: **Jesus People.**

Jesus People (or Jesus Movement): a contemporary religious movement that began in 1969, consisting of Evangelists, Neo-Pentacostalists, and Fundamentalists who lived communally, preached the gospel on city streets, and lived ascetically. Members had a deep personal relationship with Jesus Christ. Like the early

Christians, and in contrast to conventional Christians, many were willing to forego the rewards of property, status, success, and social roles, believing Jesus was their highest and only value. Many Jesus communes and farms existed throughout the United States, Canada, and the world before the movement died out in the early 1980s.

The Jewish Catalog: a famous book and "do-it-yourself kit" on Jewish creativity and traditions, compiled by three people who emerged from the Havurot movement and the Jewish counterculture: Richard Siegel, Michael and Sharon Strassfeld. In a light-hearted and joyful way, they introduce Jewish customs and rituals to essentially assimilated Jews. See: **Havurot Movement; Jewish counterculture; Jewish radicalism.**

Jewish counterculture: a spontaneous movement among young Jews, man of them students, who wished to return to a more joyous, more authentic experiential involvement with Judaism and Israel. It began in the late 1960s in the United States and spread throughout the world. The Jewish counterculture was the spiritual-traditional side; the political side was called Jewish radicalism. See: **Jewish radicalism; Havurot Movement.**

Jewish radicalism: the political side of the coin to the Jewish counterculture of the 1960s in the United States, Canada, and Europe. In essence, it was a loose amalgamation of Jewish activists who broke from the SDS (Students for a Democratic Society) and other leftist groups of the time in order to focus more attention on such issues as anti-Semitism, Zionism, Israel, Soviet Jewry, and Jewish tradition. This movement later developed into such groups as Breira and New Jewish Agenda.

Jews for Jesus: a religious sect that specializes in attracting Jewish young people into a special appreciation for Jesus Christ. They feel that one can be a "completed" Jew and a "full" Jew by such beliefs. They are similar to "Jesus People" in style. One could also view them as a Christian missionary group directed at Jews.

Jones, Rev. Jim (1938-1978): the founder and leader of the People's Temple of the Disciples of Christ cult of San Francisco. An American white man, Jones led his interracial band of followers to build Jonestown, a rural kibbutz in Guyana, but in November 1978 he induced them (over 900 people) to commit mass suicide and homicide. See: **Jonestown; People's Temple of the Disciples of Christ.**

Jonestown: the name of the agricultural farm, deep in the forests of Guyana, that Rev. Jim Jones and his followers built, and where they all died in an act of mass suicide and homicide. Today it is in ruins, forlorn and forgotten.

Journal of the Society for Common Insights: a scientific journal published by the Unification Church of Rev. Moon. Deals with issues in science and religion. Founded in 1976.

Kabbalah: Jewish mysticism; chain of inner transmission of the secrets of esotericism. The noun is Kabbalist; the adjective is Kabbalistic. Sometimes spelled Cabala or Qabbalah. The most famous Kabbalistic text is the *Zohar*, complied by Moses de Leon in the 13th century. Although based on Jewish doctrine, it has taken important elements from Gnosticism, Neoplatonism, and oriental mysticism, thus making it a work useful to both Christians and Jews.

Kagyupa Order: a sect that practices the Tibetan Vajrayana form of Buddhism. Also called the Kagyu

Droden Kunchab. The latter was founded by Kalu Rinpoche of the Kargyu Sect. Lama Lodru is the resident Lama. Headquarters is in San Francisco, California.

Kali: wife of Hindu god Shiva; Great Goddess.

Kama Sutra: Kama is the Hindu god of love, desire, and passion. Kama Sutra is a Hindu book of love and erotica.

Karma Yoga: yoga through selfless devotion.

Karma: Sanskrit term for chain of moral cause and effect or the force generated by consciousness and actions that affect this and future lives.

Kerista Village: flower tribe, utopian lifestyle on the West Coast from 1971 to 1991. Members were celibate until they joined a "Best Friend Identity Custer" and then had sexual intercourse with each member of the cluster, male or female. They also practiced a "Gestalt-O-Rama" a psychological exercise designed to eliminate inner fears and bad habits. Kerista Village had about 20 members in their center in San Francisco's Haight-Ashbury district.

Kidnap-rescue: the act of taking someone by force out of a cult in order to deprogram him. A very controversial tactic that some courts have considered illegal, especially if the victim is an adult and not in physical danger.

Koan: A Zen Buddhist riddle, used to stop linear thinking and aid in meditation.

Krishna: the chief deity of the Hare Krishna Movement; a Hindu god, considered by the Hare Krishna Movement to be *the* major god, the incarnation of Vishnu, Supreme Personality of Godhead, the wisdom of the wise, adviser to the Pandus, and singer of the Bhagavad Gita. See: **Hare Krishna Movement.**

Krishnamurti Foudation: founded by Jiddu Krishnamurti (1895-1986), Indian philosopher and writer (*The First and Last Freedom, Think on These Things, You are the World*). He is one of the most well-known of living philosophers of religion. He had schools in four countries, at one time charged $4,000 for full-term annual tuition (and got it), and marketed a full line of books, tapes and videocassettes. He had an estimated 10,000 followers and thousands more through his many books.

Kudzu: a prolific Japanese ornamental vine, also found in the southern United States, with a remarkable ability to cover everything from high-wire electric lines to cars and houses.

Kundalini Yoga: yoga that awakens the *kundalini*, the vital primordial energy at the base of the spine. This is accomplished through a series of rapid and violent breath intakes. Also called Laya Yoga.

Kushi Institute: Founded by Michio Kushi and centered in Becket, Massachusetts, it is a multi-sided organization that runs the Erewhon food stores, publishes the *East-West Journal* and holds various classes. Its philosophical basis is the application of macrobiotics to life. See: **East-West Journal; macrobiotics; yin/yang.**

Lao-Tzu (Master Lao): 7th-century B.C. Chinese sage, mother and father of Taoism. See: **Taoism.**

Leary, Timothy (1920-1996): psychologist, pioneer LSD researcher, guru and thinker. Author of *The Politics of Ecstasy.* See: **LSD.**

"litnessing": distributing spiritual material and talking to people on the street. Used by members of the Local Church of Witness Lee. See: **Local Church of Witness Lee.**

Local Church of Witness Lee: In 1962, Witness Lee (1905-1997) brought his anti-denominational, anti-Christian pulpit from Taiwan to Anaheim, California. Members burned banners reading "RELIGION" and wore T-shirts with the motto "God Hates Christianity." Lee taught that only through intuition and divine experience could one know God; the Bible and other books only confounded us. His 8,000 followers in North America and 70,000 in the Orient were forbidden to read anything except what the church printed through its Living Stream Ministry Publishing Company. Members, who had to live no farther than three miles from the nearest church (there were more than 50 in the United States at one time), donated about $1 million a year to the church.

Lomi Body Work: combines meditation, Gestalt, body therapies, and movement to allow the inherent intelligence of the body to emerge and the promote integration of body and psyche. Developed at the Lomi School in Mill Valley, Calif.

"love-bombing": to overwhelm a person with love, affection, and acceptance. Used by many cults to attract and hold new converts.

Love Family, or the **Church of Jesus Christ at Armageddon:** A one-time real estate salesman, Paul Erdman, changed his name to Love Israel and founded the Church of Armageddon in San Francisco in 1970. A year later he took his flock to Seattle, Washington. Members took new first names (Serious, Reverence, Solidity, etc.) and used the last name Israel. They observed a form of *Kashrut* (kosher food), smoked hashish, and hyperventilated. Women cut and brushed the men's hair, bowed when entering a room, and spoke only when spoken to.

129

LSD: Short for **lysergic acid diethylamide,** this is a powerful hallucinogenic drug, first synthesized by Dr. Albert Hofmann in Switzerland in 1943. Rediscovered, so to speak, in the 1960s and promoted by such American gurus as Timothy Leary and Allen Ginsberg, this drug, also called "acid," became popular with many intellectuals and those in the so-called "youth culture." After ingesting the drug (in the form of a tablet), a long, eight-to-twelve-hour "trip" would ensue with surreal results. Users could see space and time contract or expand, could manifest new personalities (such as historical figures), and watch wondrous pictorial displays. The drug is similar in chemical make-up and effects to mescaline, but much more powerful. Its use has diminished in the 1980s because of fear of contamination with other, perhaps dangerous products. See: **Ginsberg, Allen; Hofmann, Dr. Albert; Leary, Timothy.**

Lubavitcher Rebbe (1902-1994) (Actual name: Menachem Mendel Schneerson): the spiritual leader of the Lubavitcher Hasidim. He lived in Brooklyn, N.Y., where the headquarters of his worldwide Chabad-Lubavitch movement was located. See: **Hasidim; rebbe.**

Macrobiotics: Greek for "great life," this is a way of life developed by Georges Ohsawa and furthered by Michio and Avaline Kushi (now living in Brookline, Mass.), stressing a balanced whole grains and organic vegetable diet, natural agriculture, yin/yang philosophy, Oriental medicine, palm healing, Shiatsu, respect for ancestors, cultivation and preservation of traditional values in both the East and West, realization of one's personal dream, and attainment of complete freedom and happiness. See: **yin/yang.**

Maharaj-ji (1958-), a.k.a. Guru Maharaj-ji: the spiritual leader of the Divine Light Mission. He became well known in the United States as a 15-year-old spiritual leader. He has, however, fallen from favor because of family conflicts and high living, and membership has fallen off, though there are several *ashrams* and groups of the Divine Light Mission throughout the United States today. See: **Divine Light Mission.**

Maharishi University of Management: a college, located in Iowa, based on the philosophy of the Maharishi Mahesh Yogi. It offers courses in religious philosophy, the arts, and meditation.

Maharishi Mahesh Yogi (1918-2008): founder of the Science of Creative Intelligence and the Transcendental Medication Program. An Indian "guru." Author of *The Science of Being and the Art of Living* and other works. See: **meditation; Transcendental Meditation.**

mahatma: Sanskrit for "great soul"; a title of respect; for example, Mahatma Gandhi, the great leader of India.

Mahayana Buddhism: Sanskrit for "great vehicle," this is the Buddhism of the Northern regions — Tibet, China, Korea, and Japan. It stresses the bodhisattva ideal. See: **Buddha; bodhisattva; Theravada Buddhism.**

mana: awesome, silent power attached to things or people. In Polynesia, the "life force."

mandala: Sanskrit term for intricate pattern of geometric or artistic symbols used for instruction or meditation.

mantra: a spiritual chant or sound. Sanskrit for a formula composed of syllables (either meaningful or meaningless) whose sounds produce psychic or spiritual effects; a sacred sound. Mantras are given to followers by the leader to chat or meditate upon.

marijuana: the hemp or cannabis plant. A drug obtained from this plant is smoked, and a euphoric feeling called a "high" is obtained. Not considered a dangerous or addictive drug.

Maslow, Abraham (1908-1978): humanist, "third-force" psychologist who emphasized the creative, positive side of human beings and whose writings were used by the counterculture of the 1960s and 1970s to affirm their own views of the human potential in people. Maslow coined the famous concept of self-actualization. His many books include *Toward a Psychology of Being; Religions, Values and Peak Experiences; Eupsychian Management;* and *The Farther Reaches of Human Nature.*

meditation: the art and science of contemplation and concentration; reflection and doing nothing; centering the whole being; self-analysis and self-reflection; discipline of mind, awareness, and control of thoughts, emotions and states of consciousness; and simple acts with complex ramifications and uses.

megavitamin diet: a diet consisting of large doses of vitamins plus water in place of solid food. Check a doctor before starting.

Meher Baba (1894-1969): the spiritual name of **Merwan Sheriar Irani,** a Sufi master and Indian-born prophet of Persian lineage who taught Sufi wisdom and kept silent for 44 years. He has a small following in the United States and other countries.

mescaline: a hallucinogenic drug derived from the peyote plant; similar to LSD, though somewhat milder. Regarded as sacred by Mexican Indian tribes. See the works of Carlos Castaneda for a description of how the drug works. See: **Carlos Castaneda, LSD.**

Messianic Age: a concept in Judaism and Christianity wherein a perfect paradise will emerge after the Messiah appears and Armageddon is fought. It will be a time of perfect peace, perfect wisdom, and eternal life.

Messianic Jews: another term for Jews for Jesus. Sometimes called "Completed Jews." These are Jews who believe in the divinity of Jesus Christ.

metaphysical: supernatural and visionary; a branch of philosophy that seeks to explain the nature of being and reality. Certain metaphysical cultural movements included Paul Klee, William Blake, Max Ernst, Giorgio de Chirico, and Antonio Carro in art, as well as John Donne, George Herbert, Henry Vaughn, and Tom Traherne in poetry.

Millennium '73: the huge display and celebration of the Maharaj-ji and his Divine Light Mission held in Houston, Texas, in 1973. It was a dismal failure in bringing about the messianic age.

Mind/Body Duality: The mind is the faculty that constantly evaluates, judges, and reasons, while the body is the physical substance of the human, animal, or plant.

miso: a Japanese soybean paste, made by way of fermentation.

Mithras: the ancient Persian God of Light and Truth.

monastic: ascetic; characteristic of certain orders of monks or nuns; a life devoted to simplicity, order, contemplation, work, and prayer.

Moon, Rev. Sun Myung (1920-2012): the spiritual leader of the Unification Church ("the Moonies"); a Korean man whose followers thought of him as Christlike. See: **Unification Church.**

Moses David: another name for David Berg, the

founder of the American cult, the Children of God. See: **Berg, David Brandt.**

Mo Letters: religious and political directives (letters) written by Moses David to his followers in The Children of God cult.

Muktananda, Swami (1908-1982): an Indian spiritual leader and guru with a following in the United States and elsewhere.

mysticism: transcendental knowledge of God through contemplation; the belief that spiritual truth may be attained by direct apprehension, apart from intellect or normal senses.

Naranjo, Claudio: psychologist, consciousness researcher; author of *The Healing Journey.*

Naropa University: a well-known Buddhist study and religious center in Boulder, Colorado, that offers degrees of B.A. and M.A. in Buddhist theology and psychology and certificates in dance, poetics, and theater as well as classes in martial arts and music. Founded in 1974 by Chögyam Trungpa, a Tibetan Buddhist teacher and Oxford University scholar of comparative religions.

Native American Church: a Native American peyote cult formalized in 1941.

Naturei Karta: Aramaic for "guardians of the city." An extremely militant Orthodox Jewish sect found in Jerusalem and New York.

naturopathy: treating sickness through natural remedies — air, sunshine, saunas, and herbs — as opposed to drugs or medication.

Needleman, Jacob: a California professor of religion, well known for his books on contemporary spiritual movements.

Neve Shalom: a New Age community between Jerusalem and Tel Aviv.

New Age: movement devoted to making the earth a happy, safe place to live; an Aquarian Age.

New Age Journal: Published in Boston, this journal explores contemporary social and religious movements, the new psychologies, communities, and social-political events of this age.

"new games": a movement, emerging out of San Francisco, which promotes the use of games as a means of attaining fun and fellowship; of competition without bitterness and rancor; of games with no winners and no losers.

New Harmony community (1825-1827): a utopian community in Indiana led by George Rapp and later Robert Owen.

New Left (1963-1973): a radical movement devoted to participatory democracy; economic freedom; decentralization of authority; equal rights for women, Blacks, Chicanos and other minorities; and an end to imperialist wars. It differed from the "Old Left" of the Communist and older Socialist parties, who were considered too dogmatic and ideological. However, the New Left was also wracked with ideological squabbles. In response to police and FBI suppression, it turned violent and cut itself off from its student- and worker-base of support. When the Vietnam War ended, the New Left, too, died. See: **Jewish radicalism.**

Nichiren Shoshu Academy (Soka Gakkai): Based on the Buddhist teachings of Nichiren Daishonin Ikeda, a 13ᵗʰ-century sage, this movement was brought to the United States in 1960, where it now has more than 35,000 adherents. The religion attempts to change negative to positive destiny through daily chanting ("*Nam Myh Renge Ky*") before holy scrolls (called the "gohonzons"). It will also make you very rich, they say, but I daresay it is making the cult leaders quite wealthy from the sale of those scrolls.

nirvana: Sanskrit for "extinction"; cessation of attachment to desire and delusion; enlightenment; a state beyond life, death, and rebirth.

noetics: the science of consciousness and of its alterations.

nonsoul: immortal non-essence of living beings. Buddhist term.

Oahspe: derived from the exclamation "oh," the word for awe, "ah," and spirit, "espe." A book received psychically by John Newbrough concerning the history of the past 24,000 years. Also known as the Kosmon Bible, it was compiled in 1880-1881.

occult; occultism: theories and practices concerned with the attainment of secret powers of mind and spirit.

Okido: Japanese for the "way of Oki"; a school of yoga founded by Masahiro Oki.

old religion: a term for witchcraft. See: **witchcraft.**

Oneida Community: a utopian community in New York state, led by John Humphrey Noyes, from 1848-1881.

One World Family: a communal organization founded by "Allen-Michael" in Haight-Ashbury, San Francisco, in 1967; also known as the Universal Industrial Church of the New World Comforter.

orgone: a form of healing energy first discovered by Wilhelm Reich. Its has not been scientifically proven that orgone actually exists or heals.

OT (Operating Thetan): next stage after "clear" in which one is free of time and space. See: **Scientology; Dianetics.**

Ouspensky, Peter D. (1878-1947): a Russian mathematician and associate of Gurdjieff. Author of *In Search of the Miraculous.* See: **Gurdjieff.**

overmind: plane of consciousness beyond mind; creator of truth.

Oversoul: the "absolute" in Brahman tradition.

pandit: Sanskrit for "learned person".

paramahamsa: Sanskrit for "Supreme Swan," honorific title of a supreme yoga master.

Patrick, Ted (1930-   ): a Californian black man who has emerged as the most feared (by the cults) deprogrammer in the nation. He is quite successful. See: **deprogramming.**

pentagram: a five-pointed star used in occult divination.

People's Temple of the Disciples of Christ: the cult founded by the Rev. Jim Jones in California in the 1960s that built Jonestown, an agrarian farm, in Guyana, where Jones and more than 900 of his followers committed mass suicide and homicide in 1978. See **Jones, Rev. Jim.**

People Searching Inside (PSI Seminars): This southern Ontario (Canada) mind school offers courses based on Eastern mysticism and group encounter. Inward Bound IV, the four-day introductory course, is the most popular course. It is a fast-moving encounter battleground where members tearfully confess to matricide or incest fantasies, a musical theme such as Rodgers & Hammerstein's "Climb Every Mountain" is played, and after all this psychological torture, disciples are happily re-accepted into the group.

Perfect Master: a term used by followers of the Divine Light Mission to describe their spiritual leader, the Maharaj-ji. See: **Divine Light Mission; Maharaj-ji.**

Perls, Fritz (1893-1970): psychologist, founder of Gestalt therapy. A complex and fascinating man, a guru to many in the human potential movement, he spent his last years in the United States at the Esalen Institute in California. See: **Esalen Institute.**

peyote: a hallucinogenic drug used by Mexican Indian tribes.

polarity therapy: a method of correcting energy imbalances and restoring the innate sense of harmony that we call health.

Porter, Jack Nusan (1944-   ): sociologist, writer, editor; one of the founders of the Jewish radical movement in the United States in the late 1960s. See: **Jewish radicalism, New Left.**

prajna: Sanskrit for "wisdom"; seeing clearly; wisdom arising naturally from meditation, love, and compassion.

prana: Sanskrit for "life energy."

prasada: Sanskrit for "consecrated food," food that has been blessed.

Pray-reading: a form of prayer used in the Witness Lee cult. See: **Local Church of Witness Lee.**

"premie": a novice in the Divine Light Mission of the Guru Maharaj-ji; a lover of the divine in Sanskrit. See: **Divine Light Mission, Maharaj-ji.**

Primal Scream: a therapeutic technique of relieving deep-rooted experiences, developed by California psychologist Arthur Janov.

The Process (The Process Church of the Final Judgment): a cult that worshipped both Christ and Satan, on the grounds that Satan would become reconciled to Christ, and they would come together at the end of the world to judge humanity, Christ to judge and Satan to execute judgment. It was active in the Midwestern cities (Chicago), the East (New York and Boston), and England in the 1960s and 1970s. Its members wore long black robes adorned with a red cross-like insignia, and were found selling their journal in the streets. Following the removal of their co-founder, Robert DeGrimston, by their Council of Masters in 1974, the organization was renamed The Foundation - Church of the Millenium, then the Foundation Faith of the Millennium, followed by the Foundation Faith of God in 1993. The organization eventually became Best Friends Animal Sanctuary in Kanab, UT, later Best Friends Animal Society.

process meditation: meditation using a mantra out of one's own experience.

Prophet, Elizabeth Clare (1939-2009): Married to Mark L. Prophet (his real name), Elizabeth Clare (Wolf) strengthened the spiritual sect founded by her husband called the Summit Lighthouse. This sect is an amalgamation of Christian, Buddhist, Hindu and occultic practices. Mrs. Prophet was an oracle through which messages reach her followers. Headquarters are in Santa Barbara and Malibu, California. See: **Summit Lighthouse.**

proselytizing: the practice of converting a stranger into a religious follower.

psi: Actually the 23rd letter of the Greek alphabet, it also means the processes and factors in human personality or nature which appear to transcend or deny the accepted limiting principles of science or common sense; another term for ESP, or extrasensory perception.

PSI Institute: See: **People Searching Inside Institute.**

psilocybin: a psychedelic drug similar to mescaline. See: **LSD; mescaline; psychedelic.**

psychedelic: mid-expanding; hallucinogenic; a term for drugs like LSD, mescaline, or psilocybin that induce mind-expanding and sensory experiences. See: **LSD; mescaline; psilocybin.**

psychetypes: a no-blame approach to conflict resolution. The theory is called **psychetypology** and involves compromise and deep understanding.

psychic: a person who can foretell the future or has other extrasensory skills; a trance medium in the realm of the paranormal, occult, or astral.

Psychosynthesis: Developed by the Italian psychologist Roberto Assagiolli and Johannes Schultz, it is a psychological and educational means to integrating the Self, utilizing both Eastern and Western methods. Has spread to the United States and other Western countries and is used in the human potential movement.

pyramid power: an ancient form of power that allegedly resides in figures or shapes that are pyramidal; a occult system of prophecy based on various proportions and measurements of the Great Pyramid in Egypt, which are held to correlate with important historical events. Scientific Egyptology rejects such notions.

raga: Sanskrit for love; musical note or harmony.

Raja Yoga: Sanskrit for "King of Yogas"; spiritual science developed by India thinker Patanjai, emphasizing regulation and control of the mind.

Rajneesh, Shree Bhagwan (1931-1990): teacher and guru of tantric and Sufi heritage; founder of Neo-Sanyas; resided in Poona, India, with homes in the United States and elsewhere. His most famous follower was the daughter of Congressman Leo Ryan, who was killed at Jonestown, Guyana, by devotees of Rev. Jim Jones. See: **Sufism; tantra.**

Ramakrishna (1836-1886): Bengali saint and founder of movement of Divine Mother worshippers.

Rama, Swami: Indian Spiritual teacher (1903-1972); India teacher and founder of the Himalayan International Institute of Yoga Science and Philosophy in 1971.

Ram Dass, Baba (1932-   ): the guru name for America psychologist Richard Alpert. Once an associate of Timothy Leary in his LSD experiments at Harvard University, today a leader of a small sect; author of *The Only Dance There Is* and other works. See: **Hanuman Foundation.**

Rastafarians: a Black cult founded in Jamaica, synthesizing African and Biblical themes; "Rastas," as they are known, view the late king of Ethiopia Haile Selassie as their spiritual leader; the have also made a ritual of smoking powerful marijuana and wearing their hair in "dreadlocks." Several well-known reggae musicians, including Bob Marley and Peter Tosh, were Rastafarians.

Reb Nachman of Bratzlav (1772-1811): a controversial *zaddik* (Hebrew for "holy man") and Hasid from Podolia in the Ukraine. The controversy concerned his feeling that there was only one true *zaddik* or *rebbe*, in actuality the Messiah. See: **Hasidism.**

rebbe: Hebrew word for guru, teacher, Hasidic rabbi with followers who come to him for advice, both spiritual and practical; the leader of a Hasidic sect like the

Lubavitch, Satmar, and others; much more than simply a rabbi. See: **Hasidism; Lubavitch; Satmar.**

Reich, Wilhelm (1897-1957): controversial Austrian-born psychologist; broke with Freud, and emphasized the relationship of the political and the psychological; discoverer of orgone energy; was hounded and jailed in the United States during the last years of his life; author of *The Function of the Orgasm, Character Analysis, the Mass Psychology of Fascism, The Sexual Revolution*, and many other works; founder of bio-energetics and other forms of Reichian therapy. See: **bio-energetics; orgone.**

Reiki: "Universal Life Force" in Japanese. A method of laying-on-of-hands healing developed by Dr. Mikao Usui from Kyoto, Japan.

reincarnation: the rebirth into various bodies (human, animal, vegetable, or mineral) from one lifetime to the next.

Rinzai School: a Zen school founded in the 9th century by Chinese Ch'an master Rinzai Kigen utilizing koan technique; brought to Japan in 1191 by Eisai. See: **koan; Soto School; Zen.**

Rogers, Carl (1902-1987): important American psychologist and group leader; founder of client-centered therapy; author of many books including *On Becoming a Person, Freedom to Learn, and On Becoming Partners.*

Rolf, Ida (1896-1979): developer of the Rolfing technique of deep massage and manipulation of the body in order to "realign" it more harmoniously. See: **Rolfing.**

Rolfing: Named after Ida Rolf, it is a form of deep massage and maneuvering of body ligaments in order to "line up" the body. See: **Rolf, Ida.**

roshi: Japanese for "reverend master"; title of a Zen master, conferred upon the worthiest of disciples.

Rosicrucian Fellowship: a secretive, occult Christian fellowship founded by Max Heindel (1865-1919) and based on earlier sects. See: **AMORC.**

Rosicrucian: a member of a medieval European secret society professing esoteric knowledge; founded by Christian Rosenkreutz in the 15th century. There are contemporary groups based on this older sect. See: **AMORC.**

Rubin, Jerry (1938-1994): anti-war activist and leader of the "yippies" (political hippies). A member of the famous "Chicago 8" that went on trial in 1968, he later became a stockbroker and investment counselor in New York City. See: **hippies, "yippies"**

Rudhyar, Dane (1895-1985): musician, painter, astrologer, and guru/teacher.

Rudin, Rabbi A. James: a well-known Jewish rabbi, active in the American Jewish Committee on many religious issues, most prominently with religious cults and sects. His wife, Marcia Rubin, and he are authors of the book *Prison or Paradise? The New Religious Cults* (1980).

Sabbatarian: a person who strictly observes the Sabbath on Saturday, as Orthodox Jews and some Christian sects do.

Sabbateans: a sect of followers of the false messiah Sabbatai Zevi (1626-1676). See: **Zevi, Sabbatai.**

Sabbath: Hebrew term for day of rest, falling on Saturday; for Muslims, Friday; for Christians, Sunday. Some see the root of the word in the Sumerian term "Shabattu," meaning "a calming of the heart," observed every seventh day from the full moon festival for Nananar, the moon god, by the Babylonians, as a day of penitential reflection. There are also many mystical qualities to the number seven, since the Sabbath falls on the seventh day of the week.

Salvation Army: a Christian evangelical and social welfare organization, founded in 1865 by William Booth of England. Organized along military lines, this "Christian army of soldiers" combines doctrinal reality of sin and redemption along with social work with the lowest rungs of society — criminals, drunks, prostitutes, tramps, etc.

samadhi: Sanskrit for concentration or meditation.

sambodhi: Sanskrit for "perfect enlightenment."

samsara: Sanskrit (Hindu) term for the karmic chain of birth, death, and rebirth on earth according to reincarnation. Release from this endless chain of suffering can only be gained through yoga practices.

Sanskrit: the classical language of India, related linguistically to Greek and Latin; rarely spoken today.

sanyasi: he or she who prepares the Zen tea preparation. See: **Zen.**

Satanism; Satan: the worship of the devil; the god of evil.

Satchidananda, Swami (1914-2002), a.k.a. Satchidananda Saraswati: Indian teacher and guru; founder of the Integral Yoga Institute; a fine man.

Satmar Rebbe (1887-1979) (actual name: Joel Teitelbaum of Satmar): the spiritual leader of a large Hasidic sect, living in New York City. Satmar Hasidim are militantly pietistic and strongly against the State of Israel and Zionist leaders for their alleged atheism. See: **Hasidism; Lubavitcher Rebbe; rebbe.**

satori: Zen Buddhist term for enlightenment produced by meditation. See: **Zen.**

satsang: Sanskrit for "association with truth"; direct contact with the spirit of God within or through a saint; spiritual discourse; communion or company of devotees of a spiritual teacher. The term is used by followers of the Maharj-Ji's Divine Light Mission.

satyagraha: Gandhi first popularized this Sanskrit term; it is the force that is born from truth and life; nonviolence; direct action.

Schacter, Rabbi Zalman: Neo-Hasidic teacher of Jewish counterculture in the United States, Canada, and Israel. Author of *Fragments of a Future Scroll.* See: **Jewish counterculture.**

Scholem, Gershom (1897-1982): German-born, now living in Israel, Jewish scholar, pioneer and leading authority inn the field of Kabbalah and Jewish mysticism. Most well-known works are *Major Trends in Newish Mysticism* and his translation of the *Zohar.* See: **Kabbalah; Zohar.**

Scientology: Since its formation by science fiction writer L. Ron Hubbard in 1954, Scientology has grown into perhaps the world's largest cult. A religion for tax purposes, it is also a commercially packaged psychological "science" based on Hubbard's book *Dianetics.* Members take a seminar, then a 12-hour course in which encounter group techniques are used. Hubbard's E-meter, a sort of homemade lie detector, determines psychological weak points. Courses designed to strengthen these are then offered at a cost of $5,000 or more. Scientologists have been known to harass enemies such as journalist Paulette Cooper, who wrote *The Scandal of Scientology.* Eleven members faced charges recently from Watergate-like break-ins of several Washington offices (including the IRS) where files on Scientology were stored. Some 2.5 million Americans have tried Scientology, including Karen Black, Tom Cruise, John Travolta, and, during his imprisonment in the early 1960s, Charles Manson. There are an estimated 8 million graduates worldwide, and annual revenues are in the hundreds of millions. See: **Dianetics; E-meter; Hubbard, L. Ron.**

Second Death: As the soul leaves the body for further development at a higher spirit sphere, there also takes place a similar refinement of personality on passing on to the next sphere above.

Sect: a group of movement that breaks away from an established religion in order to practice a purer, more pietistic life. Similar to a cult but more acceptable and legitimate. Can develop into an established church over time.

Sefer Yetzirah: Hebrew for "book of creation"; a Kabbalistic book on numbers and letters and their mystical meanings.

Seicho-No-Le: As soon as we realize we're already perfect, taught founder Masaharu Tantguchi (d. 1985), then our lives will be perfect too. This also rules out the possibility of disease. Cancer, he says, is simply the symbol of a stubborn mind. Church members meditate twice daily. By the end of 2010, the movement had more than 1.6 million followers and 442 facilities, mostly in Japan.

Self-Realization Fellowship: Paramahansa Yogananda, who brought SRF to the United States in 1920, lived for thirty years in North America. He taught Kriya yoga and used the Bhagavad Gita plus the Old and New Testaments as scriptures. At one time there were 150 nuns and monks at SRF headquarters in Los Angeles, and thousands have taken courses offered through the fellowship's 500 temples, retreats, ashrams, centers, and meditation circles around the world. See: **self-realization.**

self-realization: the process of realizing one's own potential, of finding one's deepest spiritual or psychological needs; similar to self-actualization.

sephirot: Hebrew term for the ten creative emanations of God, constituting the existence of the world. Part of the system of Kabbalah, Jewish mysticism. The sephirot are arranged in a hierarchy from one to ten. See: **Kabbalah.**

Shah, Indries (1924-1996): a Sufi religious leader and author. See: **Sufis; Sufism.**

Shakers: groups of early American religious sects, sympathetic to the Quakers. As many as 60 groups existed in 1837. They were a visionary movement that lived communally and were non-sexist and ascetic. Active in the 18th and 19th century, they are best known today only for their furniture and folk art. The term "Shakers" came from the slight trembling observed as they became religiously inspired.

Shakti: Sanskrit for "energy"; the divine female.

shaman: tribal priest, "medicine man," originally from Siberia.

shambhala: The word has several meanings: a mythical kingdom in Central Asia where all spiritual energies emanate; a site where Buddha taught; Buddha nature, essence of all things; and a publishing house in Berkeley, California, founded in 1968.

shiatsu: Japanese form of "finger pressure"; a form of acupressure massage used for physical and mental health. See: **acupressure.**

Shrii Shrii Anandamurti (1921-1990), a.k.a. Prabhat Ranjan Sarkar: an Indian teacher founder of Ananda Marga. See: **Ananda Marga.**

Siddhartha: the given name of Buddha, referring to a period before his attaining enlightenment; title and main character of Hermann Hesse's famous novel about a disciple of the Buddha. See: **Buddha.**

Silva Mind Control: Founded by Jose Silva (1914-1999), an engineer, this is a process by which goals in life can be achieved through deep concentration, repetition, and other techniques. Very similar to methods used by "get-rich-quick" groups.

SIMS (Students International Meditation Society): See: **Transcendental Meditation.**

Sivananda Yoga Vedanta Centers: a movement to spread the teachings of the Swami Sivananda (1887-1963), an Indian doctor, yogi, spiritual teacher, and founder of the Divine Life Society.

Snyder, Gary (1930-   ): a Beat poet and thinker. Author of *Turtle Island, Earth House Hold, Myths and Texts*, and *The Old Ways.* His life exemplifies the interplay of Eastern and Western concerns.

Soto School: one of the major Zen sects brought to Japan from China by Dogen. It emphasizes natural koans arising from daily life, unity of training, and enlightenment. See: **koan; Rinzai School; Zen.**

soul: the immortal essence of all beings; the mediator between spirit and matter.

Speaking in tongues: See: **glossalalia; Xenoglossy.**

spiritual: concerning the spirit or soul; religious or sacred.

Spiritual Counterfeits Project: a group of California Christian activists who, through educational ventures, newsletters, and conferences, try to neutralize the impact of American cults by fighting religion with religion. Quite successfully, I might add.

spiritual despotism; religious fascism: absolute control of religious followers. Some cults are merely religious forms of despotism.

spiritual materialism: security-oriented ego-feeding spirituality.

Spiritualism: the science, philosophy, and religion of continuous life, based upon communication with the dead by means of mediums. It studies the laws of nature both on the seen and the unseen sides of life.

Sri: pronounced "shree." Mister, sir, polite form of address in Sanskrit.

Sri Chinmoy (1931-2007): a spiritual master from Bengal, India, credited with more than 350 books, 2,000 songs, and 130,000 mystical paintings, he also meditated daily on each of his more than 1,000 disciples around the world, who must shower, wear clean clothes, and put out flowers every day so that their images will be pleasant. Chinmoy centers teach "path of the heart" yoga and are supported by student donations.

Steiner, Rudolf (1861-1925): Austrian social philosopher and mystic; founder of anthroposophy. The son of a stationmaster, he is chiefly known for his educational system, numbering more than sixty schools throughout the world. In addition, there are more than 30 schools in England alone for the benefit of handicapped children. Steiner was greatly influenced by the German poet Goethe. He believed that human history shows an evolution of consciousness, that new faculties of cognition are still to be developed.

Stevens, John Robert (1919-1983): founder and leader from 1954 on the Church of the Living Word ("The Walk"). Had congregations in 25 states and nine foreign countries. Stevens lived in Southern California, and the church was strongest there and in Hawaii. See: **Church of the Living Word.**

Students International Meditation Society (SIMS): the youth branch of the Transcendental Meditation movement.

Suares, Carlo (1892-1976): esoteric Kabbalah author, noted for such books as *The Cipher of Genesis, The Passion of Judas, The Resurrection of the Word, The Song of Songs,* and *The Sepher Yetsira.*

Subud: a mystical movement established in 1947, stemming from the teachings of Pak Subuh (or Muhammad Subuh Sumohadiwidjojo, (1901-1987) of Indonesia. Many of John Bennett's (one of Gurdjieff's students) people formed the original core of Subud members in the late 1950s, but since then membership has come from all races, religions, beliefs, and people. In Subud, one follows no teachings or dogmas, nor does one meditate. One simply receives the Latihan, Pak's teachings passed on to his followers. Subud does not claim to be a religion but aims at the unity of all peoples in the worship of God. They do, however, reserve certain "divine mysteries" as secrets. Pak Subuh claimed revelations in his 24th year. His coming was foretold by Gurdjieff.

Sufi: an initiate of the Sufism movement, an esoteric, mystical order that developed under Islam, noted for its mystical singing, dancing (Sufi dancing), and whirling (hence the term, whirling dervish).

Sufism: Islamic mysticism; apprehension of divine realities and the renunciation of human possessions.

Sufi Order: mystical Islamic organization founded in 1910 by Hazrat Inayat Khan in San Francisco with Headquarters in Suresnes, France, and New Lebanon, New York.

Sufism Reoriented: Sufi group founded by Meher Baba in Meherabad, India, with headquarters in Walnut Creek, California, since 1952. See: **Meher Baba.**

Summit Lighthouse: This group was founded in Washington, D.C., in 1958 by Ascended Master El Morya of Darjeeling, India, for the express purpose of publishing the teachings of ascended masters dictated by the "messengers" Mark and Elizabeth Prophet. The organization is a unique example of a group that combines spiritualism, occult practice, and a mystical worldview of the East. It is quite sophisticated in its literature and promotions. See: **Prophet, Elizabeth Clare.**

Sunday, Billy (1863-1935): a former professional baseball player who turned to evangelical work in 1896. He preached widely and was very popular but heavily criticized for his unconventional methods. He was the forerunner of the TV and media evangelicals of today. The book and movie *Elmer Gantry* was based on his life.

Sunburst: On 5,000 acres purchased with a lump settlement for a back injury, Norman Paulson, a Self-Realization graduate, built a community near Santa Barbara, California, where he was joined by 350 disciples from across the United States. They said they saw visions of Paulson as a prophet. Sunburst operates food markets, a restaurant, a juice factory, a bakery, and a publishing company.

Suzuki, D.T. (1870-1966): prolific writer and interpreter of Zen Buddhism. Author of such books as *Mysticism: Christian and Buddhist: The Eastern and Western Way; Zen and Japanese Culture;* and *Zen Buddhism; Selected Writings.*

Suzuki, Shunryu (1904-1971), a.k.a Suzuki Roshi: Japanese-born Soto Zen Master; inspirer of the San Francisco Zen Center. Author of *The Zen Mind and Beginner's Mind.*

swami: Sanskrit for lord, master, spiritual teacher.

Swedenborg, Emanuel (1688-1772): noted and talented man who founded the New Church and Swedenborgianism, which is consistent with spiritualism teachings; Swedish mystic and prophet.

Synanon: started in Santa Monica, California, by a reformed alcoholic named Charles E. "Chuck" Dederich, Sr., (1913–1997), whose position was eventually worth $20 million. The 900 hard-core members were mainly former junkies, alkies, cons, and crazies who traded all worldly possessions for salvation from their addictions. Once seen as a model (though controversial) treatment center, it changed into a military-like cult. Upon Dederich's suggestions members shaved their heads, underwent mass vasectomies, undertook abortions, and divorced old partners to marry new ones. Dederich and two other Synanonites were charged with putting a rattlesnake in the mailbox of a Los Angeles lawyer who had won a $300,000 legal judgment against Synanon. The lawyer was bitten but recovered. Synanon did not. It formally dissolved in 1991. See: **Dederich, Charles.**

tae kwon do: Korean martial art, founded in the fourth century. The words mean "kick punch way."

taboo: prohibition of dangerous contact.

T'ai Chi Chu'uan: Chinese martial art based on subtle yielding, circular movement, and control of *chi* ("life energy" in Chinese). founded in the 14th century.

Talmud: Jewish book of study, containing the fundamental principles of Jewish law and consisting of a text and commentary (*Mishna* and *Gemara*). Written over a long period of time, 70-550 A.D.

tantra: Sanskrit term for a set of books utilizing the senses; meditative sexual union; spiritual science divided into four areas (ritual, meditation, conduct, and wisdom).

Tao: a Chinese word for Logos, the Absolute, the course of nature, the way, the path.

Taoism: a Chinese way of life inspired by Lao Tzu. Taoist doctrine implies a passive reaction to the world in contrast to the Confucian system of activity. It stresses nature, mysticism, alchemy.

Tarot: an ancient system of divination by use of a deck of 78 picture cards with archetypal symbols (The Fool, Empress, Lovers, Devil Stars, etc.). These symbolic cards, which go back to the 15th century, represent humankind's destiny.

Teilhard de Chardin, Pierre (1881-1955): French Jesuit, archaeologist, geologist, and mystic; author of *The Phenomenon of Man*, *Hymn of the Universe*, and *Toward the Future*.

theocracy: a government by priests or religious leaders claiming to rule with divine authority.

theocratic socialism: a form of religious socialism; spiritual communitarianism.

theology: the study of God, religious doctrine, and matters of divinity.

Theosophical Society: the society founded by Madame Helena Petrovna Blavatsky in 1875 to promote the doctrines of theosophy. See: **Blavatsky, Mme. Helena Petrovna; Spiritualism; Theosophy.**

Theosophy: a movement founded by Madame Helena Petrovna Blavatsky and Colonel Olcott in 1875. It is noted for its eclectic philosophy, world cycles, cosmic initiation, secret matters, and evolution to other planets. It teaches a doctrine of compulsory reincarnation and the development of latent psychic power. See: **Blavatsky, Mme. Helena Petrovna; Spiritualism; Theosophical Society.**

Theravada Buddhism: Sanskrit for "Vehicle of the Elders"; Buddhism of Ceylon, Thailand, Burma, and Laos. See: **Mahayana Buddhism.**

Thompson, William Irwin (1938-   ): a New Age author and thinker; founder of Lindisfarne, a community in Southampton, New York; author of *At the Edge of History, Evil and World Order,* and *Passages About Earth.*

tofu: a Japanese food and excellent source of protein; made from organic soybeans.

Torah: the Mosaic Law; the Pentateuch; the Five Books of Moses. Hebrew for "Teachings."

Transactional Analysis: a theory of group interaction developed by psychologists Eric Berne and Thomas Harris (author of the book *I'm OK, You're OK*).

Transcendental Meditation: a religious technique of relaxation developed by the Maharishi Mahesh Yogi. It stresses the use of mantras for meditation.

Transcendentalism: a literary and philosophical movement of the 19th century, stressing nature and Eastern thought. Its major figures were Ralph Waldo Emerson, the Alcotts, and Henry David Thoreau.

transpersonal psychology: a movement stressing full sensory, psychic, and spiritual development.

"trip": a 1960s countercultural term for a voyage or journey, especially one with a spiritual quest; an LSD or other drug experience.

"True Parents": the appellate of Rev. Sun Myung Moon and his wife. His followers replace their own parents with Rev. Moon. He becomes their "true parent."

Trungpa, Rinpoche Chogyam (1939-1987): Tibetan Buddhist teacher; 11th incarnation of the Trungpa Tulku, supreme abbot of the Surmang Monastery; founder of the Naropa Institute in Colorado; author. See: **Naropa Institute.**

"Turn West": opposite of "Turn East"; term used by the theologian Harvey Cox to denote those who turn to the materialist Western countries of the United States and Europe, as opposed to those who turn to the East, the spiritual emphasis. See: "East Turners."

UFO cults: UFO stands for Unidentified Flying Object, a "flying saucer" of people from outer space. UFO cults are groups of people who have allegedly encountered such aliens from another planet and have evolved a lifestyle from such encounters. For example, in April 1975, 26 people renounced their families, sold their possessions, and left Los Angeles to join up with a couple known as The Two on a UFO cult journey to the next evolutionary kingdom. The Two operated out of a post office box in Mississippi, and their 1,000 followers around the country avoided sex, liquor, and drugs and did not mingle very much with ordinary earthlings.

Unfoldment of Kenneth G. Mills: A New Brunswick, Canada-born former concert pianist, Kenneth G. Mills (1923-2004) attracted hundreds of disciples and formed a brotherhood that extended from Toronto, where he last resided, to New York, San Francisco, and Tucson, Arizona. Poet, author, musician, and philosopher, Mills lectured students in rhyming couplets and recorded several albums. His disciples saw the perfection inherent in every human being.

Unification Church ("Moonies"): one of the most
controversial cults to arise in the 1970s. A millionaire
industrialist, the Rev. Sun Myung Moon (1920-2012),
founded this church in Korea in 1954, and brought it to
the United States in 1972. His more than 30,000 devotees
called him the Messiah. Some would say that they would
die (or even kill) for him, and in one report have allegedly
rehearsed their own suicides in case such action becomes
necessary. Their bible is Rev. Moon's "Divine Principle"
which mixes Christian fundamentalism, extreme
patriotism, puritanism, and old-fashioned Americanism
into a curious yet extremely seductive concoction. Moon's
extreme wealth, his political and business connections,
and alleged tax evasions caused him to leave the United
States and his beautiful estate in Barrytown, New
York (on the Hudson River, near Tarrytown) for parts
unknown. The Church, under Mose Durst, a former Jew,
was still going strong. Its current president is InJin Moon,
daughter of Rev. Moon. See: **Moon, Rev. Sun Myung.**

Unity of Sciences: A major goal of the Unification
Church is something loosely defined as the unity of all
knowledge. Carried out by the International Conference
on the Unity of the Sciences (ICUS), the Church holds
annual conferences (the first was in 1972) with scholars
from all over the world. Young people are not the only
ones to be fooled by the "Moonies." Sun Myung Moon's
plan was to unite all sciences and all scientists under his
banner.

Universal Mind: term used by Spiritualist author
J.A. Findlay to describe mind substance as the result of
etheric vibration. It is, he says, the creative power in the
universe, and its rapidity of vibration makes it plastic.
This plasticity of mind leads to image-forming, or what
we know as thought. According to this theory, all matter
contains this thinking substance.

156

Upanishads: The second section of sacred Hindu literature, following the Vedas. It centers around the possibility of esoteric teachings to be gained by sitting close to a teacher. Three principal commentaries are by Badarayana, Sankara (800 A.D.), and Ramanya (1017 A.D.). The study of yoga has its origins in these. See: **Veda, yoga.**

Veda: the oldest section of Hindu sacred literature, the basis of the Brahmin faith. The first, the Rig-Veda, was composed around 1500-1000 B.C.

Vedanta: mainstream Hindu philosophy based on the Veda and the Upanishads.

Vedanta Society: The Vedanta movement was started in the United States by Swami Vivekananda, who came to represent Hinduism at the World's Parliament of Religions in Chicago in 1893. He founded the Vedanta Society of New York in 1896 and one in San Francisco in 1900. At present there are sixteen Vedanta Centers in the country run by monks of the Ramakrishna Order of India. Vedanta, which forms the basis of the various sects of Hinduism, is one of the major living philosophies and religions of the world. "Vedanta" means, literally, the concluding portions of the Vedas, India's most ancient scriptures.

vegetarian: one who is a non-meat eater. Vegetarianism is associated with such diverse religions as Buddhism, Jainism, Taoism, Zoroastrianism, the Essenes, Trappists, Benedictines, and Seventh-Day Adventists.

Velikovsky, Immanuel (1895-1979): an Austrian-born Jewish psychoanalyst, historian, and mythologist whose controversial reformulation of both Biblical history and astronomy is still being debated. Author of *Worlds in Collision, Earth in Upheaval, Peoples of the Sea,* and *Oedipus and Akhnaton.*

Vipassana: insight meditation; a form of sitting and moving meditation used to reduce stress and stabilize the individual.

Vishnu: Hindu deity, one of the trinity (with Brahma and Shiva); the "Preserver"; a beneficent God, said to have had a number of subhuman and human incarnations or *avatars*. Incarnated as Krishna, the charioteer, he is the divine-human spokesman of the Bhagavad Gita. Many worthy people of recent times have been considered incarnations of Vishnu by the Hindus.

Vivaxis Energies International Research Society: According to Frances Nixon of British Columbia, your vivaxis is your lifetime individual energy pattern, which forms shortly before your birth. X-rays and certain drugs interfere with the energy flow. Nixon's 1,500 followers, concentrated in British Columbia, California, and Florida, applied dried kelp powder to their bodies and used lead and cadmium inactivator boxes to restore their normal flow of energy.

Vivekenanda, Swami (1863-1902): a disciple of Ramakrishna, he was the founder of the Vedanta Societies in the West. See: **Vedanta Society.**

The Walk: See: **Church of the Living Word; Stevens, John Robert.**

Wandervogel: a mystical German youth movement of the 1920s that studied Taoism and the *Bhagavad Gita*. Hitler corrupted and bent this movement to serve his own needs, and many members later became Nazis.

Waskow, Arthur (1933-): One-time political radical, civil rights and anti-war activist, Waskow, who makes his home in Philadelphia, turned to Judaism and emerged as one of the key leaders in the Jewish radical movement and counterculture of the late 1960s and 1970s. Author of *The*

Freedom Seder, The Bush is Burning, and *Godwrestling.* See: **The Jewish Catalog; Jewish counterculture; Jewish radicalism.**

Watchman Nee (1903-1972): dynamic early teacher of The Local Church of Witness Lee in the late 1940s and 1950s. See: **Local Church of Witness Lee.**

Watts, Alan (1915-1973): Episcopal theologian, Zen teacher, influential countercultural guru in the 1960s, author of *This Is It; Beat Zen; Square Zen; Zen, The Joyous Cosmology; Nature, Man, and Woman; Two Hands of God; The Wisdom of Insecurity; Cloud-Hidden, Whereabouts Unknown; and The Book: On the Taboo Against Knowing Who You Are.* See: **Zen.**

The Way International: the religious cult founded by the American Victor Paul Wierwille (1916-1985), an evangelist and author of the book *Jesus Christ Is Not God.* Wierwille founded The Way in New Knoxville, Ohio, in 1942 and believed that God talked to him and proclaimed him "son of God." (He denied the divinity of Jesus Christ.) The cult had some surprising success in the Midwest and the South. See: **Wierwille, Victor Paul**

White Brotherhood, The Great: believed by those in the occult to be the true seat of world government by a hierarchy of Masters or Adepts. Not part of Spiritualist philosophy. (It does smack of the anti-Semitic book, *The Protocols of the Elders of Zion,* about a group of Jews who control the world.)

Whole Earth Catalog: a book catalog that described hundreds of ways to "survive" on planet Earth. It led to numerous imitations. "Whole Earth" is also an adjective that means cosmic consciousness or New Age.

Wicca: Old English for "witch." Middle English used the term "wycche," and modern English uses the term "witch." There are several theories behind the name: one from the Anglo-Saxon root *wic-*, meaning "change." It is the same root from which "week" is derived. The Anglo-Saxons used a lunar calendar, and a week is the term at which the moon changes from one phase to another. Another theory is that "witch" derives from *wit-*, a Anglo-Saxon root meaning "wise or knowledgeable," and witchcraft has traditionally been referred to as the "Craft of the Wise." See: **witchcraft.**

Wierwille, Victor Paul (1916-1985): founder and first leader of the religious cult, The Way International, which is more visible in the Midwest, South, and Mountain States than in the East or Western United States. See: **The Way International.**

witchcraft: Witches should not be considered a cult or a sect, but an ancient pagan religion that advocates nature, animal life, the heavens, and magic. Witches can do only good, not evil. See: **coven; wicca.**

witnessing: a term meaning to publicly testify one's beliefs; also to go out into the streets and seek new converts.

Worldwide Church of God: a fundamentalist Christian sect/cult with offices in many countries, including Israel. Founded by Herbert W. Armstrong (1892-1986), it was later involved in controversy between Armstrong and his son Ted and other issues, for example, the magazine *Quest.*

wu wei: Chinese term for "nondoing" or "actionless action"; a Taoist concept of ceasing to strive or attain.

xenoglossy: another term for "speaking in tongues." See: **glossolalia.**

Yahweh: Jehovah, the early tribal God and special protector of the Jews. The word is actually **YHVH,** the unspeakable and unutterable name of God.

yaza: all-night Zen meditation. See: **Zen.**

yeshiva: Jewish theological seminary; a place to study Torah, Talmud, Zohar, and other holy books.

yin/yang: ancient Chinese cosmic principle of duality, the interplay of which is felt to form the background of all human experience. Interpretation of any possible yin/yang experience is worked out by a divination technique known as the I Ching. See: **I Ching.**

yippies: a cultural and political group that arose in the late 1960s. Founded by Jerry Rubin and Abbie Hoffman, they were politicized hippies. See: **hippies; Hoffman, Abbie; New Left; Rubin, Jerry.**

yoga: ancient Hindu system of self-discipline and psychic training with the object of uniting the Lower with the Higher Self and thus attaining freedom from the otherwise inexorable round of rebirth and Karma. Many systems of yoga are available and popular today, many using it as a method of physical culture, an objective for which yoga was never intended. Some of the most well-known yoga systems are: Bhakti (devotion); Hatha (breath); Kundalini (chakras); Raja (mind control).

Yoga Journal: a journal dealing with yoga systems, techniques, nutrition, holistic health, and spiritual communities. Published in Berkeley, California.

Yogananda, Paramahansa (1893-1952): Bengali yogi; founder of the Self-Realization Fellowship in California; author of the famous book *Autobiography of a Yogi.*

yogi (male); yogini (female): practitioners of yoga. See: **yoga.**

zafu: a sitting cushion used in Zen, usually made of black cloth about 6" high and 10" in diameter.

Zalman, Reb Shneur (1745-1813): one of the early leaders of Chabad Lubavitcher Hassidim. See: **Chabad; Hasidism; Lubavitch.**

Zarathustra (628-551 B.C.): the original Persian prophet of Zoroastrianism. He resembled Moses or Mohammed as a leader, recalling his people to a purer faith, with a belief in a future life and the coming of a savior. It was, perhaps, the first monotheistic religion, similar to ones to come later. In Mumbai, India, and other places, the followers are called Parsis. (This is the Greek term for his name; the Latinized form is Zoroaster.) See: **Zoroastrianism.**

zazen: Japanese Zen concept of sitting meditation.

Zen: Mahayana Buddhist movement introduced into China from India in the 6th century and to Japan from China in the 12th century A.D. It emphasizes sudden enlightenment through spontaneous madcap behavior or paradoxical sayings/phrases (called koans). It lies at the basis for *jiu-jitsu* as well. It had a deep influence on both the Beat writers of the 1950s and the hippies/counterculture of the 1960s. See: **koan; Rinzai and Sotto Schools of Zen.**

zendo: a Zen meditation hall or room.

zenji: a Zen master.

Zevi, Shabbetai (1626-1676): Also know as Shabtai Tzvi, he was a "false messiah" who in the 17th century proclaimed himself "King of the Jews," the Messiah. He attracted a large following and was on his way to Israel when in Turkey he was arrested by the Sultan who offered him two choices: death or conversion to Islam. He chose conversion, and his most fanatical followers comprise a sect within Islam to this day. Other false messiahs followed Zevi; he was neither the last nor the only one.

Zohar: the oldest known treatise on Hebrew mysticism; it is the foundation of the Kabbalah and the Old Testament. See: **Kabbalah.**

zone healing: healing based on massage and reflex action.

Zoroastrianism: a religion and way of life based upon the teachings of Zoroaster (Zarathustra) which flourished in Persia (Iran) until the Arab conquest. See: **Zarathustra.**

ABOUT THE EDITOR

Dr. Jack Nusan Porter is a Boston sociologist, editor, writer, and religious activist. He has taught Jewish theology at Boston College, Jewish history at Emerson College, and general sociology courses at Northwestern University (where he received his Ph.D.), De Paul, SUNY-Cortland, Pine Manor College, and the University of Lowell. His published works include *Jewish Radicalism* (1973); *The Sociology of American Jews* (1978, 2nd ed. 1980); *Kids in Cults* (with Irvin Doress, 1977, 1980); *The Jew as Outsider: Collected Essays, 1974-1980* (1981), *Jewish Partisans* (1981, 1982) and numerous other works. He is listed in *Who's Who in the East*, *Who's Who in Israel*, *Contemporary Authors*, and *American Men and Women of Science*. He is married to the former Miriam Almuly of Brookline, Mass.

<u>ABOUT THE AUTHOR</u>

Jack Nusan Porter is considered one of the founders in the field of modern sociology of Jewry, modern genocide studies, and the sociology of the Holocaust, having taught one of the first courses in comparative genocide at the University of Massachusetts at Lowell in 1977; edited one of the first anthologies in the field, *Genocide and Human Rights: A Global Anthology*, in the late 1970s; and compiled the first curriculum guide in teaching the sociology of the Holocaust in 1992, *The Sociology of the Holocaust and Genocide* (published by the American Sociological Association).

He is a former vice president and treasurer of the Association of Genocide Scholars and a former Research Associate at Harvard University's Ukrainian Research Institute under Professor Omeljan Pritsak.

He is the author or editor of more than 30 books and 700 articles and essays including *The Sociology of the Holocaust and Genocide* (rev. ed. 1999), *Sexual Politics in Nazi Germany* (1995), and *The Genocidal Mind* (2006). He has also been a contributing editor to the *Encyclopedia of Genocide* and has served on the editorial board of *Internet on the Genocide* (in Australia).

A widely acclaimed author, editor and teacher, Jack Nusan Porter is considered one of the pioneers of the modern sociology of Jewry, being a founding member of the Association for the Social Scientific Study of Jewry, and the author or editor of such classic works as *The Sociology of American Jews, The Jew as Outsider,* and *Jewish Radicalism.*

He was the founder and publisher of the *Journal of the History of Sociology* and has been a contributor to the *Encyclopedia Judaica,* the *Encyclopedia of Sociology,* and *The Italian-American Experience: An Encyclopedia.*

He has taught sociology or Jewish studies at Boston University, Boston College and Northwestern University.

Born in the Ukraine in December 1944, Porter, age 69 (in the year 2014), came to America in 1946 after a year in a DP Camp in Linz, Austria, and grew up in Milwaukee, Wisconsin.

He received his B.A. in Sociology and Hebrew Studies at the University of Wisconsin at Milwaukee in 1967 and his M.A. and Ph.D. in Sociology at Northwestern University in 1971 at the age of 26.

He has lived on Kibbutz Gesher Haziv, attended school in Jerusalem at the Machon Institute for Youth Leaders, and attended rabbinical school at the Academy for Jewish Religion in New York City. He was the spiritual leader/ rabbi of Temple Emmanuel in Chelsea, Massachusetts, and of Congregation B'nai Zion in Key West, Florida, and is today an independent scholar, lecturer, and research fellow at the Davis Center for Russian and Eurasian Studies at Harvard University. He can be reached at (617) 965-8388 or at jack.porter1@verizon.net. His website is www.drjackporter.com.

January 2014

www.ingramcontent.com/pod-product-compliance
Lightning Source LLC
Chambersburg PA
CBHW022335280326
41934CB00006B/641